New Models for
Financing the Local Church

Dr. Raymond B. Knudsen is the author of

STEWARDSHIP ENLISTMENT AND COMMITMENT
NEW MODELS FOR CREATIVE GIVING
NEW MODELS FOR CHURCH ADMINISTRATION
MODELS FOR MINISTRY
DEVELOPING DYNAMIC STEWARDSHIP
THE WORKBOOK
    (A companion volume to all of the above)
THE TRINITY

NEW MODELS
FOR FINANCING
THE LOCAL CHURCH

Fresh Approaches For the
Computer Age

Second Edition

RAYMOND B. KNUDSEN

MOREHOUSE-BARLOW
Wilton

Copyright © 1974, 1985 by Raymond B. Knudsen

First published by Association Press,
Follett Publishing Company, Chicago

Second edition published by
Morehouse-Barlow Co., Inc.
78 Danbury Road
Wilton, Connecticut 06897

ISBN 0-8192-1369-1

Library of Congress Catalog Card Number 85-061217

Printed in the United States of America

2 4 6 8 10 9 7 5 3 1

To my wife Edna,
our three sons
Raymond, Silas, and Mark,
and our daughter
Ann Delight,
for whom the giving of resources
and selves is a way of life.

Contents

Preface

WHY do we need new models for financing the local church? This is a good question. The answer is based upon five premises:

- *First*, the local church is basically a cash-funded organization. Fifty-two offerings each year are for most families cash transactions for the support of mission. Though a comparatively modest amount of the church's receipts are in cash, the volume of member participation support is in cash. Envelopes for offerings are designed for cash gifts.

- *Second*, our culture is rapidly moving into a cashless society. Checks and plastic currency have become the order of the day. Few are there who do not have their wallets full of them.

- *Third*, the local church has not adapted its funding-source procedures to the climate of the check-writing period of fiscal history, let alone the bank-card period of fiscal history. In this twentieth-century check-writing era we are still operating local churches on a nineteenth-century cash-flow basis.

- *Fourth*, the machine age of technical data processing has made for a sophisticated society divorced from traditional procedures of cash flow. Computer processing for credit-debit procedures has rapidly come upon us, and it is already later than most of us think. Yet local churches are not programmed into the standard and accepted fiscal procedures of these times.

- *Fifth*, the church must adapt its funding procedures to fund transfer systems if it is to sustain its fiscal integrity and spiritual mission.

My first effort at fund raising took place in my first student pastorate, where I undertook to help my church raise $500 to be used as a down payment on a manse. Since then, adequate financial support for the local church has been a central concern in my ministry. This book has grown out of my conviction that in any local church adequate programming depends on adequate financial undergirding.

Over the past fifteen years it has been my privilege to serve the churches in their mission as the Special Assistant General Secretary for the National Council of the Churches of Christ in the U.S.A. and Chairman of the Board for the National Consultation on Financial Development in developing support from foundations, corporations, and individuals in all fifty states and many countries around the world.

This experience has made it clear that there are new models for financing the local church that can provide adequate support for a program in mission that will meet the needs of tomorrow's world. By no means are these models emerging only in large urban churches with multiple staffs. Some of the most creative experiments I have seen are being conducted in small rural churches and in modest suburban settings. Open-country churches, town churches, inner-city churches—all are faced by the same problems, and in each kind of setting there are pastors and congregations who are facing these problems with determination and with practicality. Taken together, they give me hope for the church and its mission in tomorrow's world. It is for that reason and in that hope that I share these emerging models on the following pages.

ACKNOWLEDGMENT

I would express my sincere gratitude to Robert Roy Wright, Editor for Association Press, in the preparation of the First Edition; and to Stephen S. Wilburn, Editorial Director for Morehouse-Barlow Co., and Raymond B. Knudsen II, President of the National Consultation on Financial Development, for their assistance in the preparation of the Second Edition.

New Models for
Financing the Local Church

1

The Changing Climate

IN 1963 MR. FRANK FISHER, vice-president of the County National Bank, conducted me through their new facility. Magnetic code numbering had been introduced for deposit forms and checks and the newest computers had been installed to facilitate the transfer of funds between accounts and between banking institutions across the land. With pride Frank said: "We are almost at the place when you can write a check in Los Angeles and it will be reflected in your account here in New York the very same day!" I replied: "Frank, that is not the kind of bank I am looking for!"

Probably none of us, really, are looking for this type of bank. We have all written checks in one town with the knowledge that they would not reach our bank to be charged against our account for at least three days. Now such transactions may take only three or four seconds. Yet this is only the latest step in a revolution that has been going on over the past few decades in our daily financial lives.

Fifty years ago employees of most firms would receive their total earnings in cash each week and proceed to make the rounds of the butcher, the baker, and the candlestick maker. At that time workers received their pay in full and had full discretion over all of it. Today the withholding principle has emerged as a dominant factor in determining spendable income. There is a considerable difference between the worker's total earnings and his take-home pay. Typical payroll deductions include Federal, state, and local

1

taxes; Social Security; retirement payments; hospitalization, medical care, life insurance deductions; and, in some cases, union dues. Some employees even arrange annuity investments with their employers on a withholding basis.

Even after what we have left of what we earn has been deposited to our bank account on payday, we discover that we have still less money at our discretion in the bank. Because of standing orders we may have placed with the bank cashier, mortgage payments, interest, taxes, and insurance may be debited automatically against our accounts at specified times. In fact, an officer of our Federal Reserve System reports that the average person retains discretion over only 43 percent of his net income. Payroll deductions and so-called automatic fund transfers make up the difference. One generation has seen discretion over moneys shrink from 100 percent to approximately 43 percent. And the end is not yet in view. In fact, it is estimated that by the end of this decade individuals' discretion over earnings funds will be reduced to less than 5 percent of their incomes.

What is bringing this change about? There are two important factors:

First, the present procedure for checking accounts is too bulky, time-consuming, and expensive. It costs too much to run our checking accounts as we have in the past.

Second (and even more important), the present system is wasteful of capital. It is estimated that nineteen billions of dollars are being used by Mr. and Mrs. America, businesses, and organizations without interest or service fees. As an example: one person's payday is on Friday of alternate weeks. This person will issue checks, not entirely within the law, on the Wednesday preceding payday. This is really an advance against anticipated funds, for which the banking institution receives no interest. It is no wonder that Frank Fisher was delighted with his new computer system. By providing for the immediate transfer of incoming funds, and by making impossible this system of involuntary and non-interest-bearing loans, he was able to utilize the bank's funds to the fullest, to the advantage of the bank in the first instance, and in due course for the betterment of mankind. The potential of newfound capital through facilitation of procedures is almost beyond imagination.

There is still another aspect to this problem of unused capital.

Many people carry considerable sums of money on their persons. In a recent meeting of four hundred average citizens in a metropolitan center a survey revealed that each had on his person an average of $40. Forty dollars in the purse of each of four hundred persons totals $16,000. This is $16,000 out of the reach of financial institutions. Sixteen thousand dollars of idle money. These funds could provide capital for a small business, financing for a scientific research project, or a mortgage for a modest home. Multiply this sample by the millions of people across these fifty states and the potential for capital resources is astounding.

This is the reason that plastic currency is rapidly becoming the order of the day. It is not difficult to see that we are almost at the end of the check-writing era. When I use MasterCard or VISA, or any of the other plastic currencies, the stores in which I make my purchases have transfer of funds from my account or line of credit to their accounts the same day. The retailer pays a fee for this service, to be sure, but even so his costs are reduced considerably from those incurred in charge-account procedures involved when purchases are made on a deferred plan. Immediate transfers of funds are effected through the bank card, and this bank card is certain to take the place of the checkbook and cash-on-person in the future. Mind you, in less than ten years!

Project this trend into the future as it relates to a young, recently married couple. They apply at their local bank for a line of credit, which will be granted on the basis of their lives in relation to the experience of others, and will take into consideration family life-style, education, professional proficiency, expanding experience, projected illnesses, pregnancies, etc. This is really only one step beyond the "automatic loan" feature many banks now offer in conjunction with checking accounts. The homes they will buy, the cars they will drive, their travel and living status will be determined by this line of credit. And after forty years they will have in their files 480 monthly statements providing a financial biography of their life's worth. In all this time, as the system develops, they will probably have handled less than 5 percent of their income in cash.

Interesting? Of course. Probable? Without a doubt. Wonderful? Perhaps. In a sense it becomes a totalitarian system based on economic procedures rather than political innovation.

Love So Amazing

Witherspoon United Presbyterian Church
5136 North Michigan Road
Indianapolis, Indiana 46208

MINISTRY AND MISSION

THE BUILDING FUND

The startling question in all of this is: Where is the church? If, in over forty years, this couple will have discretion over only a few dollars, how much will they give to their church? They may contribute regularly now. But as their disposable cash flow becomes ever more limited, it is almost inevitable that they will contribute less and less to the church unless the church is programmed into these energizing fiscal procedures.

One church persuaded several professional families to arrange for funds to be transferred to the church treasury from their personal bank accounts on a quarterly basis. Had it not been for this procedure their support of the local church would have been minimal. In fact, due to the demands of their professional lives and their heavy travel schedules, which make church attendance erratic at best, they may not have supported their church at all. Financial procedures had to be programmed into their economic way of life. This fact of life for these families will become the norm for most families in the future. Individuals must be educated to program the church into their financial procedures or one day soon we will find ourselves confronted with penniless churches in a cashless society.

Name _____

IN RESPONSE TO
LOVE SO AMAZING

I/We announce our intention to contribute the sum of $ _____*
to the Operating Budget each month over a period of ten quarters
beginning July 1, 1982.

____ Please process my/our gift(s) through AUTOGIVE as an electronic debit against my/our checking account. (A check marked
VOID is enclosed.)

____ Please process my/our gift(s) through my/our _____
Bankcard, Number _____. Expiration Date _____

*Opportunity will be provided to each donor to adjust their financial commitment for funding
Ministry and Mission to accommodate inflation in January 1983 & 1984. (Authorizations through
AUTOGIVE and Bankcards may be revised or terminated at any time.)

MINISTRY AND MISSION

Name _____

IN RESPONSE TO
LOVE SO AMAZING

I/We announce my/our intention to contribute the sum of $_____
each month to the Building Fund of the Witherspoon United
Presbyterian Church over a period of ten quarters beginning
July 1, 1982.

____ Please process my/our gift(s) through AUTOGIVE as an electronic debit against my/our checking account. (A check marked
VOID is enclosed.)

____ Please process my/our gift(s) through my/our _____
Bankcard, Number _____ Expiration Date _____

(Authorizations through AUTOGIVE or Bankcards may be revised or
terminated at any time.)

THE BUILDING FUND

This form was prepared by the author utilizing denominational
material.

ADJUSTMENT FOR INFLATION

New Haven United Methodist Church

630 LINCOLN HIGHWAY EAST   •   NEW HAVEN, INDIANA 46774

NOW THANK WE, ALL, OUR GOD!

    In response to the call of Christ, and in expression of my/our faith in Him, I/we will increase my/our commitment to the 1981 Operating Budget by

10%_____   15%_____   20%_____   Other:_____

Name:_____

Address: _____

City/State/Zip: _____ Phone:_____

In the event the Finance Committee does not receive your card by Nov. 10, 1980, it will be assumed that your commitment may be adjusted by 15% as we enter 1981.

    The above form has been designed by the author for parishes in the Ten Quarter Commitment Process.

    Figures utilized in the Fall of 1983 were:
       5%_____   10%_____   15%_____   Other:_____
       November 10, 1983   10% as we enter 1984.

    Figures utilized in the Fall of 1984 were:
       3%_____   5%_____   10%_____   Other:_____
       November 10, 1984   5% as we enter 1985.

    There have been many complications in working out procedures that will allow the church and voluntary organizations to relate to the new fiscal practices in our times. Statutes differ from state to state and this complicates the procedures for such organizations. As an example: In the state of New Jersey a family may take their pet to the veterinarian and arrange for prescribed medication. The prescribed medicines can be programmed through their bank card. However, the services of the veterinarian must be paid for in cash or by check.

In some states individual churches can, and have, made arrangements with their local banking institutions for contributions from members to be programmed through their bank accounts. In each case it must be done at the request of the donor and with the concurrence of the organization and the banking institutions involved. An August 1973 ruling by the U.S. Attorney General has now made this kind of arrangement possible, and there is every reason to expect that it will become increasingly common in the future.

Church executives are becoming aware of the rapidity with which our fiscal system is changing and the importance of structuring for new procedures. Some of the most exciting pioneering work is taking place in the Massachusetts Diocese of the Episcopal Church.

First, arrangements have been made by the diocese so that, as funds are deposited in local banks by local parish treasurers, the portion due the diocese is credited to the diocesan accounts at the moment of deposit. It is no longer necessary for the diocesan treasurer to wait for a local parish treasurer to write a check for the transfer of funds to the denomination, and to send it through the mails.

In a second interesting development, the diocese now pays the more than two hundred telephone accounts of the individual parishes and the diocesan offices by a single transaction from the diocesan account. This saves two hundred dollars a year in postage alone.

This is only the beginning. It is not difficult to predict that similar plans—as well as others not now dreamed of—will be adopted by other denominations as rapidly as can be managed. The church at last may come of age as fiscal procedures behind stained-glass windows keep pace with the trends of Wall Street.

There are of course real questions concerning the extent to which this trend may or ought to go. Some suggest that the move to centralized funding of diocese, presbytery, or conference should be made with all possible speed. This may well be a tragic mistake, however. It seems to be a law of life that the farther systems move from localities and persons the less effective they become and the less interest they stimulate in those who should be involved in the organizational process. Certainly there are things that can be done in concert, and through systems, in the denominational structure to provide efficiency and economy. And, again, there are matters that should be handled exclusively by the local parish.

Insurance programs are often structured on a district basis for increased economy. In the Presbytery of Hudson River of the Presbyterian Church (USA), group insurance is possible for church properties. Participation in the master policy of the presbytery makes for sizable savings to the respective parishes. In the State of New Jersey it is now possible for employers to provide their employees with group insurance coverage for real estate, personal property, and automobiles. If the denominations are alert to this potential, think of the economy this will provide for organized religion in the Garden State.

Salaries, too, may be programmed on a presbytery, diocesan, or conference basis. This would do much to elevate the bargaining strength of clergy and staffs and might well make for uniformity in salary schedules. It would also make for greater regularity in the payment of salaries, which all too often are subject to variation as volunteer treasurers act in good faith, in their own good time, to remunerate the servants of the church.

Whether we think of cash, checks, bank cards, or preauthorized electronic funds transfers, it cannot be stressed too strongly that the ultimate factor is stewardship commitment and response. As has been suggested, taken by themselves these newly emerging techniques may simply mean an increasingly greater distance between fiscal command and the church treasury. We shall also need to take advantage of new procedures, even electronic methods, to relate the individual's financial resources programmatically to the mission of the church in a positive, regular, and meaningful way. Person-to-person relationships will make the difference. Informed and committed persons will do the right thing. Enrollment in the computer system, a knowledge of procedures, and personal contact with members to ensure commitment to Christ and His Church and the implementation of procedures for funds transfers will all be required if we are to help people complete the circle of Responsible Christian Involvement.

Another side of the coin is tax reform. In the past the churches in the United States have become accustomed to a most favorable tax climate. Within recent years many changes have come, however, and today the climate is less favorable than at any time in our national history. The twig is bent. The trend seems certain to continue and the umbrella of tax shelter will shrink in size. Conditions are less favorable for the church today than prior to the current Tax Reform Acts.

A quarter of a century ago it was lawful in most states for churches to own property without tax penalty, not only for the purpose of extending their mission programmatically but also to enhance their financial position. This is illustrated by the fact that most churches, educational institutions, and nonprofit organizations had sizable investments in business and investment properties. The University of Chicago was one of the great slum lords of the period. Any property held by the church or similar organization, though used for secular purposes or investments, was exempt from taxation. Real estate was a profitable investment for these groups.

A tremendously significant pattern emerged when it was determined by state and local governments that only those properties used exclusively for the benefit of religion, education, and health programs would be exempt from real-estate taxes. This changed the investment portfolios of nonprofit organizations tremendously as investments in real estate were turned into investments in securities for which the income largely remains exempt from taxation.

Similar changes have also been taking place on state and local levels. For example, the tax status of houses of worship and residences for pastoral ministries is still generally favorable. But here, too, the climate is changing. In 1945, the law in Cook County, in the state of Illinois, was changed to provide that such a residence would be exempt from real-estate taxes only if it was indeed contiguous to the church edifice. The property would not qualify for tax exclusion if it were only adjacent to the church. In one parish the residence of the clergy was kept eligible for tax exemption only because a cloister was constructed between it and the church. In another parish the residence of the student assistant pastor, adjoining the church, was exempt, while the residence of the ordained and installed pastor, removed six blocks from the church, was placed on the tax rolls.

New Jersey law provides that no more than two residences owned by a particular parish and occupied by clergy as pastors may be exempt from taxation. The First Presbyterian Church of Tenafly was required by an appellate court to pay taxes on one of its three manses because of this law. The number of clergy compared to parish membership is never a consideration. One church with three thousand members may have four ordained staff and own four residences for them to reside in. But only two will qualify for tax exemption. Seventeen churches with membership totaling three thousand may run seventeen homes—one residence for each church—occupied by clergy and each of them will be tax exempt, although the congregations of some requiring pastoral care may number only a half dozen souls.

We could give illustration after illustration across the United States indicating that rising costs of government are causing many municipalities to rethink the privileges that religious organizations have under the traditional tax-exclusion structure. In this respect it is truly later than we think, with opinion in this direction being expressed both within and without the church. Many people insist that tax exemption and exclusion provide a state subsidy for religion and that the true separation of church and state requires no benefit whatsoever be given to organizations for religious purposes. Others take the position that a church must fulfill its obligations as a good citizen to the community in which it lives. What will this mean in the future? Within a quarter of a century all properties owned and used by the church may well be subject to taxation as earned income. This is the face of the future.

These changes will place tremendous weight upon the property and investments of religious organizations. If this trend persists, it seems probable that they will be unable to carry the burden of taxes and fixed expenditures. Church properties may well become the properties of municipalities by default. As behind the Iron Curtain, many of them may become cultural palaces, museums, and recreational centers, although it is only fair to say that many people question the validity of such a projection.

If property and investments held by religious organizations are taxed, it is reasonable to assume that the pattern of taxable income for individuals will change as well. Today a sizable portion of what we give to religious and charitable organizations is deductible for income-tax purposes. If religion becomes a taxable commodity, contributions to religion will not come under the umbrella of exclusion and exemption.

Periodically the House Ways and Means Committee of the U.S. Congress gives consideration to revenue issues. For years individual taxpayers have been expected to assume a 3 percent base, or floor, for medical costs covering medical insurances, medications, physicians, surgeons, etc. Expenditures for these must now exceed 5 percent before there is tax relief.

This formula for medical expenses has been suggested as appropriate for charitable contributions. If this should become law, only contributions exceeding 5 percent of adjusted gross income will qualify for tax exclusion. But only 8 percent of such contributions exceed this 5 percent limit! This means that 92 percent of the funds presently contributed to local churches in the United States—now tax free—would become fully taxable. It would be difficult to put a dollar value on the cost of this procedure to the local church. Certainly this would reduce, and in some cases eliminate, the tax incentive for many contributions.

It is important to the life of every local church that we sustain the tax benefits for charitable contributions we now have. In the event they are not sustained, it is important that we begin to develop every source available to provide adequate resources for the present trusts and endowments. There is no other way to ensure our capability in mission for the future.

Taxwise, it is later than we think!

The future of organized religion in our society is not so assured as many suppose. We must periodically survey the trends in our financial life that will help us scan the face of the future. We must take advantage of every opportunity for financial development if we are to ensure the church's mission tomorrow.

2

Some Preconceptions That Need Puncturing

RECENTLY A GRADUATE STUDENT serving on the staff of Riverside Church in New York City sat across from my desk and explained his need for a grant of $10,000 to fund the church's program on "Death, Dying and Aging." He hoped that I would guide him to a foundation executive who would be willing to hear his story and write a check for him all in one afternoon. He was much disappointed when I outlined funding procedures through foundations, including the fact that he sat perhaps twelve to eighteen months from a granting date.

I suggested to the young man that he explore resources within the church. He responded with many excuses: First, the church was operating on an austerity budget. Second, a recent drive for social justice had drained all the members' resources. Third, the staff was convinced that resources had to be secured from outside sources.

His second excuse was the one that gained my interest, for it is an excuse that is used frequently and wrongly. That people have responded to a need with financial support does not imply that they have exhausted all their resources. Few, if any, have given their all. Such a program in a local church is of great value not only because of the funds it provides to the particular cause but because it identifies persons in the parish who are concerned with the church's needs and have developed the art of giving. Because they have developed the art of giving, they will continue to give to good and deserving causes.

If you have a parish that has engaged in a meaningful stewardship program you have reason to rejoice because among those
who gave, you will find those who can be challenged to respond
to the deserving needs in the parish, across the nation, and around
the world. Their registered participation in previous programs
is the key to their identity and provides the base for new ad-
ventures in fund raising. The records of past financial campaigns
will not yield the names of those who have given their all, although in any campaign there may be a few who really have
done so. Rather the records will provide identification of those in
the parish who are generous, and educated and experienced in
good stewardship. Therefore, among those who had given to, and
made commitment for, the Fund for Social Justice in Riverside
Church, the young man would undoubtedly find a large proportion of those who would support his particular project in the
same church.

Visit any parish in America and you will discover that it is
always those who give to the most urgent needs in the parish that
can be counted upon to go the second mile in giving to related
causes if these causes are logical, reasonable, and justifiable.

The president of a Midwestern church-related college for the
past twenty years has a remarkable record in financial development. His experience, however, is unique because most of his
funding sources are in the immediate area. He is the first to confess
that he has not done well away from home. The Eastern Seaboard
has provided practically nothing to his administration.

When he assumed office he became involved in community
affairs. There has not been a single financial campaign in the community, either Protestant or Catholic, in which he did not play an
important part. Most of the campaigns have been successful. In
turn, he ascribes the success of his administration in funding to his
involvement in these campaigns. The ordinary reaction would be
to say that this involvement provided a list of those whose funds
were exhausted. Actually it provided knowledge of those who had
resources to share and who were willing to share their resources for
deserving causes.

• The first wrong assumption in funding is: Those who have
given to a cause have given all that they could give, would give,
and will give.

• The second wrong assumption is: People just do not have money to give.

We live in an affluent society. Even what we think of as poverty levels have advanced to the highest point, dollarwise, in our nation's history. A larger percentage of our population is economically self-sufficient than in any period of human history. The gross national product is far beyond the most optimistic projections made two and three decades ago. Our commercial products are advertised through the mass media on the premise that people have the resources to buy, do buy, and will buy if properly motivated. And yet, most of the products promoted for purchase through television certainly are not essentials. These products are developed, promoted, and distributed because the purchasing power is real.

In Ruskin, Nebraska, there are approximately two hundred inhabitants. More persons lie buried in the community cemetery than reside within the corporate limits of the town. There had been a railroad depot at the turn of the century, but it would take a detective or an archeologist to find its remains today. There is no theater, chain store, or supermarket. The total commercial area is little more than a wide place in the road. The neophyte fund raiser would say: "There is no money there." But there is a Lutheran church in Ruskin that would be an asset to the finest development in suburbia—a real architectural gem a dozen years old. In truth it is the only really fine building in the town. Someone punctured the preconception that there was no money in Ruskin and built one of the finest churches on the Nebraska prairie.

A study of the reports on per-capita giving among the Christian denominations in the United States is revealing. When the various denominations are ranked according to the per-capita worth of their constituencies, the Episcopal Church is at the top of the list. The Presbyterian (USA) and United Methodist memberships come a close second and third. But in terms of per-capita giving, the members of these three communions are far down the line. The conservative churches with a pentecostal bent and blue-collar appeal stand head and shoulders above the elite of our denominations.

People do not have money to give! How often we assume this as a basic truth. Yet individuals filing income-tax returns in 1980 reported contributions totaling $47.74 billion, and those reporting adjusted gross income under $5,000 gave 5.82 percent of their incomes, or an average of $291 each to approved charities. There is money and a willingness to share in every sector of our society today. "The fields are white unto harvest."

• A third erroneous assumption in funding is: All that people have to contribute they already contribute to their local church in the Sunday offerings.

If the parishioners are challenged to give to something else, the clergy almost universally assume that such giving will come out of the offering plates, when no assumption could be further from the fact. As a result pastors tend to guard their members with their lives, unfortunately, at their own expense and at the expense of the Kingdom of God.

Few members give really generously to their local church and few give as much as they can. The best way to increase their support is to broaden their interest. As their interest increases in the denomination, the conciliar movement, and church-related agencies, their interest increases in the local church. As their giving to concerns beyond the local church increases, their giving to the local church increases as well.

Who are the most generous contributors in our churches? The most generous contributors in our churches are those who support home and foreign missions, Christian Education, the church-related colleges and seminaries, and the councils of churches. They are those who have gained a vision of the church beyond themselves and are dedicated to an extension of their lives through it. Their generosity had its inception in the local church. Their generosity grows with experience beyond the local church, and the particular parish benefits from it.

There are classic examples across the church in every community where the stewardship response has been most unusual. Frequently they are in unique situations arising out of the particular mission of a single church. Parishes that have relocated; rebuilt after a flood, fire or accident; discovered a meaningful mission challenging fully the lives of their constituents as they have responded to community development or change. Parishes that have engaged in the resettlement of refugees from Vietnam and Cuba, discovered mission in housing and self-development, exercised faith in evangelism and human rights. Parishes that have organized institutions of higher

SELECTED DENOMINATIONS RANKED IN ORDER OF PER CAPITA GIVING

Communion	Year	Inclusive membership	Total contributions	Per capita inclusive membership
Missionary Church, Inc.	1982	25,371	$ 21,424,759	$ 844.46
Evangelical Mennonite Brethren Conference	1982	2,047	1,717,632	839.10
Seventh Day Adventists	1982	606,310	436,315,372	719.62
Evangelical Mennonite Church	1982	3,832	2,717,400	709.14
The Wesleyan Church	1982	105,221	67,786,439	644.23
The Evangelical Covenant Church	1982	81,324	51,430,402	632.42
Free Methodist Church of North America	1982	70,657	43,108,027	610.10
Church of God (Anderson, IN)	1982	184,685	102,068,406	552.66
Presbyterian Church in America	1982	149,548	82,492,076	551.61
Baptist General Conference	1983	129,928	67,360,787	518.45
Church of the Nazarene	1982	498,491	256,278,102	514.11
North American Baptist Conference	1982	42,735	21,900,467	512.47
Mennonite Church	1982	101,501	51,564,612	508.02
Christian and Missionary Alliance	1982	204,713	93,802,000	458.21
Conservative Congregational Christian Conference	1982	26,008	11,804,680	453.89
Presbyterian Church in the United States	1982	814,931	333,890,073	409.71
Church of God General Conference, Oregon, IL	1982	5,781	2,282,735	394.87
The United Presbyterian Church in the U.S.A.	1982	2,342,441	835,665,706	356.75
Churches of God, General Conference	1982	34,241	12,090,868	353.11
Reformed Church in America	1982	346,293	102,089,085	294.81
Church of the Brethren	1982	168,844	47,908,983	283.75
The Episcopal Church	1982	2,794,139	778,184,068	278.51
Reformed Church in the United States	1982	3,710	961,274	259.11
Wisconsin Evangelical Lutheran Synod	1982	412,529	99,390,243	240.93
Church of the Lutheran Confession	1982	8,986	2,077,448	231.19
Evangelical Congregational Church	1982	39,710	9,087,769	228.85

Evangelical Lutheran Synod	1982	20,025	4,572,799	228.35
Christian Church				
(Disciples of Christ)	1982	1,156,458	261,486,499	226.11
Southern Baptist Convention	1982	13,991,709	3,114,675,160	222.60
United Church of Christ	1982	1,708,847	376,463,260	220.30
Friends United Meeting	1982	59,338	12,931,395	217.93
Cumberland Presbyterian				
Church	1982	97,813	21,303,543	217.80
Moravian Church in America				
Northern Province	1982	21,618	4,289,679	198.43
The United Methodist Church	1981	9,457,012	1,794,706,741	189.78
The American Lutheran Church	1982	2,346,710	436,859,309	186.16
Lutheran Church in America	1982	2,925,655	518,781,783	177.32
American Baptist Churches				
in the U.S.A.	1981	1,621,795	267,977,722	165.24
The Latvian Evangelical				
Lutheran Church in America	1982	13,526	1,793,000	132.58

Source: The Commission on Stewardship, The National Council of the Churches of Christ in the U.S.A.

learning, rehabilitation facilities, and organizations for spiritual nurture. These are but a few illustrations of ways in which parishes have increased vision, enlarged sights, and made articulate their special mission in decisive times.

• The fourth wrong assumption is: Only the rich engage in estate planning and ordinary people cannot be expected to include the church in their wills.

The fact is that everyone engages in estate planning. Every deposit in a savings account, every payment of an insurance premium, every investment in securities and payment toward a mortgage is estate planning. The trouble is that most estate planning is accidental.

Through many years, often when invited to serve on a particular committee or in unique tasks, my father would say: "I have more time than money." Experience proves the contrary. To my knowledge I have never conducted a memorial service for a person who did not have more money than time. Time ran out before their resources did.

In most instances local church programs for cradle-to-grave planning bring dividends within a relatively short time. Thus the assumption that only the affluent are engaged in estate planning

STATISTICAL SUMMARY OF DONOR GROUPS

	Small donor (%)	Large donor (%)	Super donor (%)	Composite donor (%)
Men	23	35	42	28
Women	51	41	32	46
Couples	18	19	19	18
Under 25	1	0	0	0
26-34	4	3	3	4
35-50	17	13	14	16
51-64	31	31	34	32
65 and over	45	50	48	46
Married	49	41	48	47
Widowed	23	24	14	22
Separated	1	0	1	1
Single	21	28	30	24
Divorced	5	6	5	5
Office Worker	6	9	3	6
Management	6	6	5	6
Housewife	19	11	12	16
Sales	2	4	1	2
Professional	6	6	11	7
Service/Maintenance	1	2	3	2
Farmer/Rancher	1	1	0	1
Teacher	3	2	4	3
Own Business	3	2	6	3
Clerical	5	3	7	5
Retired	38	47	39	40
Missionary Work				
Ranked First	66	72	79	69
Ranked Second	23	19	16	21
Ranked Third	11	10	5	10
Parish Ministry				
Ranked First	35	29	26	32
Ranked Second	44	54	51	47
Ranked Third	22	17	22	21

Source: Ralph W. Sanders, Executive Vice-President "World Neighbors." *Fund Raising Management* (April 1985).

and that so-called Deferred Giving Programs cannot prove rewarding in the immediate future is completely erroneous.

• The fifth wrong assumption is: Once a commitment is made the task is done. Whether a one-time cash gift or a pledge commitment over a period of years, it is important to sustain stewardship over lives to assure donors that the decision to give or to commit funds was a proper decision, a decision worthy of being carried out.

In the commercial advertising field we learn that a primary function in advertising is to sustain the conviction in the consumer that a decision to buy was a wise decision. "Aren't you glad you bought a Buick?" reassures the buyer and nine out of ten times he will buy Buick again. "I was glad when they said unto me, let us go into the house of the Lord" encourages one to worship again and again.

Often we suffer attrition in the church because we do not sustain programmatically the decisions parishioners have made in the selection of a church, pastor, leaders, and design for service. We need to impress parishioners with the conviction that the decisions made were wise decisions. The parish that is convinced of the validity of its corporate decisions will move from one success to another in stewardship commitment programs as its horizons broaden with new vision for each tomorrow.

3

Foundation in the
Every-Member Canvass

EVERY STRUCTURE has a base. Whether we deal with traditional procedures or new models for financial development, the base in the local church is the Every-Member Canvass. With it we may be able to make only limited progress, but there is apt to be no progress at all without it. A review, then, of the canvass procedures in a local parish is a good place to begin.

Ordinarily when we talk about an Every-Member Canvass there is a tendency for church leaders to spread a series of commitment forms across the table and say: "This is what we did last year." And that is not enough. If the canvass is to realize its full potential, the local Stewardship Committee needs to start with a review of the entire process. The total experience of previous years must be assessed and assimilated if the committee is to gain a full view of approach, commitment, and fulfillment.

The purpose of this mission is to establish a profile for every family, member, and prospect. A personal family record should be prepared for each giving unit in the parish. Listed individually are the names, addresses, and positions in family life (husband, wife, son, daughter, grandparent, etc.) A glance will reveal the family potential, including information concerning those gainfully employed, in school, attending college, disabled, or retired. An approach for support will be entirely different in terms of age, dependents, educational involvement, and stage of progress in professional development and career. One person's primary stewardship may be aged dependent parents, a crippled mate, or an exceptional child. Another person's primary stewardship may be a college or trade-school education for their young people. These responsibilities are not either subordinate to or above Christian mission. Instead, they are parallel. Rather, a part of the whole. Family responsibilities are a part of the picture and must be evident in the overall view.

An important part of this profile will be the committee's best estimate of the family's financial status. The specific community in which the family resides provides some evidence of this. Other relevant data would include type of employment, length of residence in the community, and membership in the parish. The local Chamber of Commerce or Association of Commerce and Industry—and a local bank—can usually provide an estimate of the annual family income of those living in the community.

Included, as well, must be the family's experience in the parish: (1) involvement in offices, leadership, organizations, church school, and service; and (2) the financial commitments they have made each year they have been members of the parish and the amount they have paid toward each commitment. Through the year or years they may well have responded to other needs— Lenten Offerings, Building Programs, One Great Hour of Sharing, etc. All these need to be included in the profile in order to discover the earnestness of faith, the depth of commitment, the vitality of the hope that lies within. Paper commitment is meaningless to both communicant and parish.

Attendance records, both with regard to Sunday worship and individual organizations within the church, are important factors in the profile. The completeness of this part of the profile will vary drastically. Some parishes provide for a registration of attendance every Sunday, while others take the roll only on Communion Sundays. But these practices are still comparatively new in the church and certainly not universally used. Sunday-school attendance records often go back many years, however, and these may become a part of the picture as well.

If you are beginning a comprehensive program you must assimilate from the past as much as you can to provide the profile you need in each situation. If no records are available, your most meaningful progress in financial support may be two or three

FAMILY INFORMATION CARD 19 ___

NAME: _____

ADDRESS: _____

TEL.: _____

Visitors: _____

Home ___ Est. Value $ ___ Apt. ___ Est. Rent $ ___

Family Members:

	Occupation	Family Situation A	Church Membership B	Church Attendance C	Estimated Income D	Weekly Pledge	Pay-Up E	Misc.
Mr.								
Mrs.								
Birth Year								
Children								
Others in Household								

KEY:
A W=Widow/Widower   S=Single   D=Divorced   CS=College Student   Y=Youth
B CM=Church Member   NM=Non-Member   CS=Church School
C 1=Regular   2=Half-time   3=Seldom   4=Never
D a=$25,000+   b=$15,000+   c=$10,000+   d=$5,000+   e=Under $5,000
E +=Greater than pledge   R=Regular pay-up   —=Less than pledge

Simple profile form to use in hard-copy processes.

years in the future as new experience forms the base for intelligent action.

When profiles are completed to the best of your present ability, you are in a position to begin a meaningful process related to the Every-Member Canvass itself. A first step in a new canvass should be the process of organizing the member-family profiles so that like will be with like in parish life. Sort the profiles into classifications on a long table. Depending on the size of the congregation, it may be convenient to use as many as ten classifications with three sections to each labeled *Generous, Supportive,* and *Nonsupportive.*

The ten classifications are: 1. Young families without dependents. 2. Young families with dependents. 3. Mature families without dependents. 4. Mature families with dependents. 5. Mature families with dependents in college or trade school. 6. Mature families with young adults at home. 7. More mature families without dependents. 8. Single and young. 9. Single and mature. 10. Single and more mature.

The average congregation will require 10 percent of its membership to provide an adequate number of teams to visit like with like—that is, like with like so far as the categories are concerned. However, not like with like so far as the three sections in each category are concerned. The 10 percent, if possible, should be drawn from the generous sections. Supportive givers may be used as canvassers if necessary. In practice, it may be necessary to stay within the sections. If so, names should be assigned so that the more generous call upon the generous, the generous upon the more supportive, the more supportive upon the less supportive, and the less supportive upon the nonsupportive. In assigning calls the general principle is easily stated. The greater should call upon the lesser; never the lesser upon the greater.

Counselors/visitors making visits must be thoroughly trained, well informed about the church and its program, the budget and needs, and thoroughly acquainted with the Master. Their personal commitment must be made before they make their first call.

Any successful canvass must be planned around the fact that we have become a TV culture. Evening programming has become almost a thing of the past as clergy say that people will not leave their homes at night. The energy crisis also makes people more stay-at-home conscious even on the weekend—except at the time of the Every-Member Canvass! Church members who always stay home are seldom home when the visitors call for stewardship commitment. In this event, canvassers should probably return for three visits. Even so, when the results are in, as many as one-third of the calls may not have been completed. It is too late then to take a significant action that—if taken at the proper time—could have made the difference between meeting or failing to meet a budgetary goal. Before the canvass has even begun, the local governing board should resolve, and announce, that all commitments will be considered open-end commitments until notice to change or forbid is given to the financial secretary. Those, then, who have not been visited will be counted on to sustain their support at the level assumed in the preceding Every-Member Canvass. Such an action should be taken six months before the canvass and should be announced on four Sundays and published twice.

It is further recommended that a form be prepared providing the opportunity for each parishioner to respond with an adjustment for inflation or personal giving. It is appropriate that an announcement be made that the Budget Committee will structure the budget for the ensuing period with a designated percentage of increase in the event the form is not returned to the church office by a particular date. Such a suggested form is provided on page 6.

Advance commitments are important. Many canvassing experts believe that the commitment of the pastor should be made first. The measure of pastoral support should be a matter of public record. Then the commitment of the official governing family—vestry members, elders, deacons, and so on—unanimous, generous, committed. A dollar figure may be announced as committed by the pastoral leadership. A dollar figure, with percentage of increase over last year, may be announced as committed by the elders as a group, the deacons as a group, the trustees as a group, and by whatever other board, by whatever name, responsible for leadership in the parish. It is important to add to these the commitment from those participating in the Every-member visitation who are not members of the official boards. A sizable portion of your objective is thus announced as having been attained before the first doorbell is even pushed. The official family—board members, pastoral leadership, officers—supplemented by others required to make the 10 percent of the membership involved in teams for every family visitation will provide 75 percent of the figure representing total membership contributions in the preceding year and probably 50 percent of the budget goal for the present objective. All things being equal—and often they are not—a well-defined canvass with trained canvassers and based on these principles should increase support by 50 percent! Those who say: "We tried, and it didn't work!" cut corners, and the shortcuts limited their success. Every corner cut reduces support. Every shortcut limits response.

It is important to sustain a high level of commitment, with enthusiasm, from the first announcement to the pushing of the last doorbell. Progress alone, in commitment of faith and resources, will sustain the effort with enthusiasm and joy long after the pledge payment period begins.

Once an Every-Member Canvass has reached this level of proficiency, it is time to give thought to the measure of support that should be used. Almost invariably it will still be the smallest unit of printed currency. But this must be rethought. A six-year-old grandson said: "You can't buy much with a dollar any more, Grandad." This is as true in the church as it is in the market place. In no place does a dollar march with greater dignity than in a church! It doesn't buy much any more. It buys less than half as much as it did seven years ago. Inasmuch as there is a tendency for many to pledge the smallest, convenient, honorable amount—that is, a dollar—the practice is growing of seeking pledges in terms of units of support.

When the United Presbyterian Church in the U.S.A. launched its Fifty Million Fund in the sixties it took a new stance in church support that enabled the denomination not only to reach its goal of fifty million dollars committed over a period of three years but to raise the sum of sixty-seven million dollars. This new stance consisted of two things: First, a unit of support. Second, a monthly remittance procedure.

• A unit of support was pegged at five dollars per month for thirty-six months. Communicants were urged to pledge one, five, ten, twenty-five, fifty or more units a month. The most modest commitment in monetary currency on a weekly basis would have been a dollar a week—fifty-two dollars a year. The most modest commitment in unit support was five dollars a month—sixty dollars a year. For modest contributors the end result of unit support was eight dollars more than for dollar-a-week givers in a particular year—twenty-four dollars over the three-year commitment period. Even more important, a basis has been laid for increased giving.

Unit support deserves consideration. For many, a unit support of five dollars will seem convenient and desirable. For most, perhaps, the unit of support should be defined in terms of ten dollars instead. Measure the need by the capability of the parish and define the unit in terms that are compatible with the capability of the majority of your people.

VALHALLA UNITED METHODIST CHURCH

In response to the call of Christ to serve people throughout the world and with a desire to share in the work of my church

I intend to provide _____ Units* of support each month over the next ten quarters.

Name _____

Address _____

City/State/Zip_____
  Process through:
  MasterCard _____ VISA _____

	Card Expires
Charge Card Account Number	Mo.	Yr.

Signature: _____ Date: _____

- This commitment may be revised at any time by calling the Church Office.
- This commitment is to be adjusted to the inflationary index each January beginning in 1980.
- If you prefer a personal visit, please retain this card.

Thirty-month pledge card for giving based on support units, with open-end option, designed by the author for the local parish.

• The monthly commitment was the second innovation that ensured the success of the Fifty Million Fund. How many items in your family budget do you pay by the week now? The newspaper boy and the church are usually the most obvious answers. Bank payments are by the month. Mortgage payments are by the month. Utility payments are by the month. Insurance payments are by the month. All easy payments are by the month. All fiscal procedures are in tune with this fiscal timing. But not the church! Units of support may bring your church into step with fiscal timing. Adequate support requires this timing. Preparation for fiscal change in the computer age makes it imperative.

Presently, packets of envelopes are distributed to members for the convenience of presenting and processing the offering. But this tried and true means of support needs careful rethinking. Fifty-two is probably the number of weekly envelopes provided. However, fifty-two seldom get to church. Social studies consider regular attendance as twenty-six or more Sundays a year. Twenty-six spells half time for me and causes many anxious moments for the treasurer and treasury. Packets of twelve seem more logical. Even then something is missing.

I visited the second largest manufacturer of church-offering envelopes in the United States recently. The printing plant itself was a model of efficiency. One hundred envelopes were imprinted with each impression of the press. But later, when I examined the envelopes for thirty-seven hundred churches, I was amazed to discover that while the name of the church appeared on every one, not one single envelope included a mailing address! No street! No zip code! Yet over the last dozen years of my own pastoral ministry more than half of our weekly income was brought to church by Uncle Sam's mail service. And we hadn't printed our address on it, either. More would have come if we had considered the aged, the confined, and the out-of-towners. Some didn't remember. Some didn't know. Some found it inconvenient to seek the address out. We were careless stewards and our carelessness contributed to their carelessness and to the impoverishment of our mission.

In seeking unit support for a local church, a set of fourteen envelopes, adequate in size to accommodate a check and imprinted for mailing, seem to be suggested. They need not be postage paid, although a postage-paid permit is granted for a small fee by the

United States Postal Service and may merit consideration for your parish. Certainly some will take exception to it. Others will appreciate the convenience of your not requiring a stamp. Commitment need not be measured by the facility with which checks may be mailed; it can be measured by the content of the envelope.

The Fifty Million Fund, to which I referred previously, was successful in raising sixty-seven million dollars. The five-dollar unit of support was a part of the success story. The monthly gift was a part of the story. The three-year commitment was a part of the story as well. Those contributing regularly did not stop at thirty-six. They went all the way. The four extra envelopes compensated for part of the attrition normal in the program. Fourteen envelopes in your twelve-month packet may do the same. The size is important, too. Mailing regulations require an envelope larger than the size used by most churches. Ninety percent of the members of our churches contributing their offerings through envelopes must fold their check or dollars three times to make it small enough to be placed inside. Little wonder that the church receives so many quarters! A quarter slips in as slick as a whistle! Easily—because we don't seem to be asking for very much!

Traditionally, Every-Member Canvasses have preceded the fiscal year and the duration of the pledge commitment has been for twelve months. To adopt the open-end commitment is to make it possible for pledges to be sustained in the event that families cannot be reached by visitors to assure credibility in budget planning. Those planning the stewardship program have opportunities for creative programming to maximize results over the long run. Too often we tend to plan from week to week or from year to year, giving little thought to the long-range program and needs of the local church.

But with the same amount of canvassing energy it is possible to seek a commitment for a period of twelve months, a commitment for twelve months with an open end, or an open-end commitment. The second is perhaps the best of the three choices here. Open end alone may seem too long a commitment. Twelve months with open end suggests a continuation beyond twelve months, but opens the door for reduction or termination before the twelve months go by. While the opportunity is real, few take advantage of it. The twelve-month commitment, without open end, can place planning

337   OCT 14 1979   337

Valhalla United Methodist Church

200 Columbus Avenue
Valhalla, New York 10595

Amount $ ....

Please bring or send your offering regularly. If you are absent, remember the church expenses go on just the same.

Church-Budget, Salem, Ohio

Accept my gift of $..   Date ....

NAME ....

Charge to my: ☐ MasterCard
               ☐ VISA

| Card Expires | |
| Mo. | Yr. |

Charge Card Account Number

SIGNATURE ....

Illustration of offering envelopes (reverse side accommodates bank cards), designed for the parish by the author.

in chaos if a sizable percentage of the responsible membership cannot be reached in a particular canvass by an important deadline.

There are two approaches that are preferable to either of the three above. The first is a commitment for ten quarters. The second is a commitment for ten quarters with open end, establishing a base for a year-round stewardship program.

• A ten-quarter commitment, again with open end to be announced six months before the termination of the pledge period, has several advantages. First, those recruited for visitation and training as visitors are invited to serve in an effort that will not be repeated again next year. They will be more attentive to the need, receptive to training and consider their task of greater importance because the funding program is to underwrite the parish mission in three calendar years. Second, the same season of the year is not necessarily the best canvassing season for all people. A fall campaign this year will provide, after ten quarters, that the subsequent campaign will be held in the spring of the third year hence. Some feel more generous and responsible in the season of Thanksgiving and Advent. Others, for whom the heavy obligations of winter are over, or nearly concluded, find opportunity to share more generously in springtime. The ten-quarter program over a decade will tend to maximize income potential on the extended commitment schedule.

The second approach, a ten-quarter commitment with open end, establishing a base for year-round stewardship, is the option preferred above all others. Such an approach introduces a new element of flexibility into the financial life of the local parish. It does not require the canvassers to make the rounds of the entire parish at the same time nor does it make essential that every parishioner consider a commitment in each calendar year or in any defined period of time.

Suppose your parish were to have a year-round Stewardship Committee with a dozen or two dozen fully trained and committed visitors. Visitations could be scheduled in stewardship planning to provide the maximum potential for their particular efforts. One church in a Midwest industrial city is so constituted. When labor negotiations are concluded, and increased salary and benefits provided to the employees, visits are made on member families reaping the benefits. When teachers and other employees of the Board of Education have an increase in salary schedule or move up the increment scale, visits are made to them. As the years go by they have disciplined themselves also to give consideration to 10 percent of the membership at the bottom in terms of support and involvement. As they advance in commitment, others occupy the area of emphasis and the church erases fewer names from the roll than any parish I know.

The Stewardship Committee should not be concerned with the stewardship of financial resources alone. Spring visits emphasize summer opportunities in terms of vacation church school, camps,

IAO CONGREGATIONAL CHURCH

2371 Vineyard Street

Post Office Box 1050

Wailuku, Maui, Hawaii 96793

AS AN ACT OF WORSHIP....

I enclose the sum of $_____
I announce my intention to contribute the sum of $_____
each month.
___Process my gifts through AUTOGIVE with my bank account
debited on the 20th day of each month for the sum
listed above. A check marked "void" is enclosed.

Authorized Signature _____
Please Print Name _____
Address _____
City/State/Zip _____

IAO CONGREGATIONAL CHURCH
(808) 244-7353

Designed by the author for the local parish. These wallet envelopes are provided to the members, placed in the pews, and one is included in one issue of the parish newsletter each month.

and conferences. Summer and fall visits emphasize the church school, youth programming, the choirs, and continuing education. The winter emphasis is in terms of confirmation and Lenten devotion. The stewardship of life is equal to the stewardship of resources and all is of vital importance.

Whatever timing schedule is adopted in stewardship programming, there are important guidelines that apply in all:

• Select persons who will complement the mission of the Church.

• Use visitors who have a thorough knowledge of the program and needs and are completely committed to their Lord and the parish mission.

• Match visitors and prospects as carefully as you can. A woman working as a hospital maid discontinued her support of a local church because a visitor assigned to her family drove up in a Cadillac and thought that a dollar-a-week pledge was not worth his time.

• Encourage visitors to be firm but not brash, positive concerning program virtues and not argumentative.

• Retain a comprehensive report of each call to be added to the family profile for subsequent work.

• Where contacts have been favorable and productive, each visitor and prospect assignment may be sustained. When there are negative readings or a shadow of a doubt, make another assignment the next time around.

Some new models are included here. Others will be presented in succeeding chapters. But our first concern must be to provide a firm base of support in the Every-Member Canvass. Only in this way will we have the courage to venture forth in truly new directions for financing the local church.

4

Budget Building
for Increased Support

THE LOCAL CHURCH'S annual budget plays a crucial role in the life and work of the typical parish. In fact, most of what will be accomplished in the mission of the church is defined in the description and statistics of the annual projection and review.

Each year the budget is used in two ways: First, the budget, in projection form, is used to assist the members, through the Every-Member Canvass, to envision what the business of the church is and what dreams the administration holds for the new year. Second, the budget is used in connection with the annual report meeting to determine the health of the organization and to measure the success of the administration in attaining its objectives of the preceding year. While the budget *is* used in these two ways, it is seldom used effectively, and it usually does not serve its purpose in the way the leaders intended.

The budget should be seen, first, as a prime tool in the Every-Member Canvass. Often stewardship executives have encouraged churches to use an open-end budget. They insist that people should be confronted not with a budget figure but with their capability to support the cause of Christ as the Lord has made them enablers through the talents, time, and circumstances provided them. While this philosophy is good, we seldom reach our objective, for the individuals concerned know that the appeal is made for general budget support and the need is pretty well defined by the pattern of the previous year. While a person's net worth may well double in a single year, if only by an inheritance, it is not likely that such an individual will double his support to the local church budget even if that support has been inadequate when measured against his former capability. There is a possibility of project support here certainly, but not of a meaningful increase in his support of the ordinary budget.

With inflation we know that the average budget figure must increase substantially each year just to sustain the program and effort of the preceding year. Over ten years this means that the church with a present budget of two hundred and sixty-five thousand dollars is doing no more than it did thirteen years ago with one hundred thousand dollars. How difficult it is to raise two hundred and sixty-five thousand dollars when it accomplishes the same as was provided by thirty-seven percent of the amount in past years! Of course, incomes have increased as well. But we are in a different arena when we deal with people's incomes and when we deal with their willingness to support the local church. Automobiles have a bigger wallop in inducing support than do the basic needs of a local congregation.

How do we overcome the obstacle of last year's budget with a percentage increase? Elsewhere we discuss project giving. This is one answer. In terms of the total parish we must somehow encourage every person to experience the project philosophy. For the sake of illustration, let us suppose that an official board submits a budget for the new year in an amount exactly 5 percent more than the figure announced from the preceding year. In looking over the itemized budget it appears identical except for the fact that the price is higher. There is little incentive to respond to such a budget with increased support. Yet, in truth, each of us knows that however similar the budgets for the two years may appear to be, they are not the same. The same repairs and improvement will not occur. The same curricula will not be used. In most line items there will be shades of difference. Some even of great importance. The budget allocations may be the same, but in the new year it may be repair of the steps leading to the sanctuary instead of last year's repairs on the stage of the parish house. The first step, then, is to review the projected budget with an eye to discerning the new and the different, that which is an improvement over the past. Define those and announce them.

The style of the projected budget to be used in connection with the Every-Member Canvass could well be an eight-column document. In the first four columns should be placed the projected budget and the annual report of expenditures for each of the three full preceding years. Column Five can convey the projected budget for the present year, and Column Six the expenditures for the first three quarters of the present year. In Column Seven should be placed the projected budget for the ensuing year. Column Eight should be reserved for those figures representing new items, important additions, changes from the present and previous budgets.

A change in the repair budget has already been mentioned. Last year it was the stage in the parish hall. This year it is to be the steps to the sanctuary. Repairs are significant, important, and catch the imagination of people much better than does just the same figure for a comparable number of repairs or improvements as have been made in the preceding year.

Now, while new items in the budget should be made articulate, there is an element of risk here, for enhancing the visibility of such items means that they will be subject to appraisal and criticism. On occasion someone will reduce or terminate his support because of them. This is a risk that you cannot avoid, and in the long run it is well worth while in terms of the potential gain in overall support. On the other hand, the usual major items in the budget should be presented in as general terms as possible. There are always some who feel that a completely itemized budget must be shared in detail with the congregation on the basis that the people have a right to know. They do have a right to know, but in knowing they must at least be helped to make the transition from an individual to a group, from a family and home to a parish and church. The telephone bill, for example, is frequently a bone of contention. People who pay eight dollars a month find it hard to understand why a church should pay eighty dollars a month for telephone service. When they see the heating item they may respond by complaining that the custodian keeps the building too warm. Hence the importance of defining the budget in more general terms. As an example, do not list the salary of each person on the staff, but instead list an item for salaries and related costs. Do not list an item for each utility, but list an item for utilities collectively. The fewer things there are to attack in a budget the greater the opportunity to gain a reasonable commitment from people.

This projected budget should be distributed as broadly as was the comparative budget used as the financial report and should be made available to those who are not members but have become a part of the parish community through their personal involvement or the involvement of members of their families. In many churches today this distribution to concerned and interested friends exceeds in number those required for the membership itself. A part of the reason is that ours is an increasingly mobile society. Many who are engaged and involved in the church's mission never actually identify with the local institution as members.

Now consider the budget in terms of the report to the annual meeting of the parish. Few items will appear in report form as they have appeared in the projected budget preceding the report meeting by fifteen to eighteen months. Changes have had to be made along the way. Increases came that were not expected. Emergencies abound. The report budget should reflect these, with an adequate explanation of what has happened. If, in fact, you have spent $5,000 more on repairs than had been anticipated, someone will accuse the administration of favoring a relative who is a contractor if the needs and allocation have not been made explicit. I have never seen a budget overexpenditure approved without enthusiasm, however, where a good job of interpretation has been done.

Let us remember that when we come to the report meeting and a review of budget expenditures, we do have the commitment from our members for the new budget, but in few cases will that commitment have as yet been met. In the majority of cases the pledges are still to be paid. It is, therefore, as important that the parishioner be pleased with the budget report of the past year as that he be pleased with the projected budget for the new year in the Every-Member Canvass. If members are displeased with the budget report of past expenditures it is likely that donors will not be enthusiastic with support in the current year. Donors must be pleased with both. All of us can recite the names of persons whose giving has increased after the budget report meeting because they were favorably impressed with the good stewardship of the administrative staff.

Some consideration needs to be given to the form of the budget as well as to its distribution.

The projected budget, as well as the annual financial report, represents the business of the church as a corporation and institution. It will be surveyed by the keen minds of business people in the parish and parish community. The format and content should be consistent with the reports read daily by such persons. In the financial report let there be a ten-year comparison as in the annual reports of corporations. Give the members an opportunity to evaluate the progress of the church from a single overview and gain insight into its mission.

Leroy E. Eide, when Western Regional Secretary for the Stewardship Council of the United Church of Christ, never visited a church in the Western Region without carrying with him the ten-year overview of that congregation in terms of stewardship, membership, and mission.

The long view is essential to planning for program and development. This may make for disappointment under certain circumstances. But it will provide a full report to the congregation of the fiscal health of the institution. And it will answer some questions concerning the administration, the program, and the effectiveness of the institution in local, regional, national, and world mission. It is at least possible that many a federation or merger would have taken place five years earlier than it did, with an even greater advantage in mission, had the handwriting on the wall been made evident, as such a report would have done, to an understanding and concerned congregation.

Similarly, where phenomenal growth has taken place, thought would more likely be given to finding sufficient staff for program, the opportunity for enlarging mission through satellite operations, and a more thorough examination of the direction of the institution by a well-informed people. Remember, an informed people will do the right thing! We are not always convinced of this in the church, but the premise is fully as valid in the ecclesiastical as in the secular world.

These financial reports should have broad distribution in the parish, the concerned and involved business interests in the parish community, and a copy should be placed in the hands of every practicing attorney and trust officer who will be dealing with parish members in the ensuing year. Included in the report should be the forms for designated and undesignated bequests. Need I

Significant Statistics on Giving and Incomes, July 1984

Church Giving

Denomination	1970[1]	1982[2]	Up	Inflation (%)[3]	True Yr. (%)
American Baptist	132,323,701	267,977,722 (81)	102.5%	148.3	− 3.8
American Lutheran	177,018,350	436,859,309	146.8	163.5	− 1.3
Disciples	116,057,724	261,486,499	125.3	163.5	− 2.9
Episcopal	248,702,969	778,184,068	212.9	163.5	+ 3.8
Lutheran Ch. America	211,914,250	518,781,783	144.8	163.5	− 1.4
Missouri Synod Luth.	241,162,986	543,926,002	125.5	163.5	− 2.9
Presbyterian US	138,621,698	333,890,073	140.8	163.5	− 1.8
Reformed Ch. America	39,414,784	102,089,085	159.0	163.5	− 0.4
United Ch. of Christ	182,183,056	376,463,260	106.6	163.5	− 4.4
United Methodist	819,945,000	1,794,706,741 (81)	118.8	148.3*	− 2.5
United Presby. USA	357,091,885	835,665,706	134.0	163.5	− 2.3

Giving Requirements in Constant Dollars

Inflation compounded from 1970 through 1983 (14 years) = 173%
For every $1.00 budgeted in 1970, must have $2.73 in 1984 to stay even.

If you had a $ 25,000 budget in 1970, must have $ 68,250 in 1984.

$ 50,000 $136,500
$ 75,000 $204,750
$100,000 $273,000

Statistics Affecting Giving

1. In 1982, 67% of Americans claimed church membership.
2. Church attendance has varied less than two percentage points since 1969:

   1939: 41% of all Americans (55% of all Members) attended Church in typical week.
   1940: 37%
   1950: 39%
   1958: 49%
   1960: 47%
   1970: 42%
   1980: 40%
   1982: 41%

3. Church attendance is vital to contributions, due largely to the patterns of support which have been encouraged. (One gives when one attends. Less likely to give when do not attend. Offering Plate has been the encouraged medium for church support.

*Twelve years, all others thirteen years. (1) *Yearbook of American Churches*, 1972. (2) *Yearbook of American and Canadian Churches*, 1984. (3) Compounded percentage changes, Consumer Price Index, U.S. Bureau of Labor Statistics.

Sources: Department of Commerce. National Consultation on Financial Development.

remind you to include the names and addresses of the administrative officers, the staff and the trustees?

It is always perplexing to see the number of local churches that have not been convinced of the importance of an annual audit. In some cases it may be appropriate that the audit be prepared by a duly appointed or elected committee. If so, the method of selection and a listing of the persons so named should be included with the published budget and audit verification. It is most reasonable that church finances be audited by a qualified and reputable firm. Often local churches do not receive sizable grants and bequests because, deep down, potential donors question the financial integrity of the organization. No church can afford this luxury. No voluntary organization can endure temptations that may confront those handling resources if there are not reasonable and proper checks and balances in financial procedures.

An audit may replace a treasurer, give integrity to an institution, provide new resources to the organization, and save a soul.

Further distribution should be made to absentee members, namely, those residing in distant cities, the alumni (don't forget those who have been raised in the church and those who were most active in the program at the time they resided in the community), and those mentally alert but confined to rest homes and retirement communities.

The kind of financial report outlined here should be a separate document, apart from the reports shared in most parish bodies by the secretaries and treasurers of the several organizations, clubs, societies, and classes. These are important but should be kept in proper perspective in the total life of the church. They should be distributed primarily in the parish as information for the concerned in the fellowship. The annual financial report, as a formalized document, is a report to the "stockholders" of the corporation. In a very real sense of the word this is actually what they are. And they deserve a report worthy of that status.

So far we have looked at the budget only in terms of itself. But the good budget builder will want to take an additional step. Now we need to ask how the budget looks in relation to the financial resources of the community. What indices can we use in average situations across America to assess potential and assure success in financial development programs? The answer is that there are several:

- *First*, the index for potential budget support for the local church. It is reasonable to assume that a local parish can and will, all things being equal, support a local church budget equal to 3 percent of the adjusted gross income of its membership. The local Chamber of Commerce or a similar organization will have available the average family's annual income level for each community and area in all fifty of our states. Simply multiply this figure by the number of family units related to the parish to arrive at a reliable estimate of the adjusted gross income figure for the membership. Three percent of this figure is reasonable for annual budgetary purposes.

For example, suppose that the average family income for your community is $25,000 per year and that there are eighty-four family units related to your parish. This means that the adjusted gross income figure for the particular parish is $2,100,000 per year. A reasonable local church budget expectancy would be 3 percent of the total, or $63,000.

- *Second*, the index for special major gift support in the local church. Statistically speaking, in every parish there is at least one person or family disciplined enough in its giving to "save a third, spend a third and give a third." Therefore, there will be at least one giving unit capable of sharing in one gift more than the annual budget giving of an entire parish. In fact, on the average there is one such person or giving unit for each forty giving units in the average parish today. They are capable of major special gifts in project support. Thus, as an illustration, a local church might expect an annual budget of $63,000 and the possibility of three gifts totaling an additional $126,000.

- *Third*, the index for capital funds programs. Experience has shown that the average parish has a capability to match local fund giving, over a period of three years, for capital funds or improvements. A local church with a budget of $63,000 per year is capable of raising $189,000 over three years for capital funds. If those capable of major gifts are included in such an effort, it would be possible for this church to undertake a capital funds program of $567,000.

GROWTH OF PER CAPITA INCOMES
BY STATE COMPARED WITH INFLATION

State	Average per capita income 1970	1984	1984 per capita if held to inflation at rate of 184%	1984 incomes exceeded inflation by
Alabama	$2,892	$ 9,981	$ 8,213	21.5%
Alaska	4,638	17,155	13,172	30.2
Arizona	3,614	11,629	10,264	13.3
Arkansas	2,791	9,724	7,926	22.7
California	4,423	14,344	12,561	14.2
Colorado	3,836	13,742	10,894	26.1
Connecticut	4,871	16,369	13,834	18.3
Delaware	4,468	13,545	12,689	6.7
Washington, DC	4,644	16,845	13,189	27.7
Florida	3,698	12,553	10,502	19.5
Georgia	3,300	11,441	9,372	22.1
Hawaii	4,599	12,761	13,061	− 2.3
Idaho	3,243	10,174	9,210	10.5
Illinois	4,446	13,728	12,627	8.7
Indiana	3,709	11,799	10,534	12.0
Iowa	3,643	12,090	10,346	16.9
Kansas	3,725	13,319	10,579	25.9
Kentucky	3,076	10,374	8,736	18.8
Louisiana	3,023	10,850	8,585	26.4
Maine	3,250	10,678	9,230	15.7
Maryland	4,267	14,111	12,118	16.4
Massachusetts	4,272	14,574	12,132	20.1
Michigan	4,041	12,518	11,476	9.1
Minnesota	3,819	13,219	10,846	21.9
Mississippi	2,547	8,857	7,233	22.5
Missouri	3,077	12,129	8,739	38.8
Montana	3,395	10,216	9,642	6.0
Nebraska	3,657	12,280	10,386	18.2
Nevada	4,583	13,216	13,016	1.5
New Hampshire	3,720	13,148	10,565	24.4
New Jersey	4,684	15,282	13,303	14.9
New Mexico	3,045	10,330	8,648	19.4
New York	4,605	14,121	13,078	8.0
North Carolina	3,200	10,758	9,088	18.4
North Dakota	3,077	12,461	8,739	42.6
Ohio	3,949	12,314	11,215	9.8
Oklahoma	3,341	11,745	9,488	23.8
Oregon	3,677	11,582	10,443	10.9

Pennsylvania	3,879	12,343	11,016	12.0
Rhode Island	3,878	12,730	11,014	15.6
South Carolina	2,951	10,075	8,381	20.2
South Dakota	3,108	11,049	8,827	25.2
Tennessee	3,079	10,400	8,744	18.9
Texas	3,507	12,636	9,960	26.9
Utah	3,169	9,719	9,000	8.0
Vermont	3,712	10,692	10,542	1.4
Virginia	3,677	13,067	10,443	25.1
Washington	3,997	12,728	11,351	12.1
West Virginia	3,038	9,846	8,628	14.1
Wisconsin	3,712	12,309	10,542	16.8
Wyoming	3,672	12,586	10,428	20.7

NB: In 50 of the 51 areas INCOMES for the period EXCEEDED INFLATION!

Source: Department of Commerce Statistics

Programs of this type should not be placed back to back. However, a comprehensive Every-Member Canvass for local support should be scheduled at the termination of the pledge-payment period for capital funds. If so, it is possible to increase annual budget income by 75 percent. A local church with a budget of $35,000 and a capital funds pledge-payment program ending after three years should be able to increase its level of support from $35,000 to $63,250 per year.

These figures and projections do not take into account the factor of attrition in long-term capital funds programs. Such campaigns are commonly launched on the assumption that the effort is fully funded when commitments attain the goal. To proceed on such an assumption is almost to guarantee that the parish will need to engage in an extended pledge-payment program going over into the fourth and fifth years of what was intended as a three-year effort.

Shortfall, or attrition, in a three-year program will average 15 percent the first year, 10 percent the second year, and 5 percent the third year. Suppose that the objective is $100,000, which is to cover building and finance charges. There will probably be an attrition of $15,000 the first year, $8,500 the second year, and $3,825 the third. At the end of the three-year period an average congregation involved in such a program, without shortfall or attrition built into the plan, will face a deficit of $27,325. Thus, as a precautionary measure, the pledge objective ought to exceed the cost of construction and financing by approximately one-third.

There are many reasons for shortfall: We are in a mobile society and families move. Many consider their obligation to retire with their movement from the parish community. Some die and most religious organizations consider that the obligation terminates with the demise of an individual. (Legal statutes will support an effort to collect from an estate, but the element of good will among heirs is usually considered more important than collecting the debt.) Situations among persons change in terms of health, employment, and family need. Some merely responded to an effort with momentary enthusiasm; for that reason the incidence of default is greater in the first and second years of the three-year campaign.

If such a shortfall expectation is not built into a capital-funds program from the very beginning, the indebtedness remaining at the end of the first pledge-payment period will seriously handicap the fullest financial development of the parish. For it has the effect of forcing the parish to conduct a second such drive back to back with the first. And experience has shown that six years should elapse between major capital-funds or building-program campaigns. This, in turn, means that it will not be possible to conduct a comprehensive Every-Member Canvass for normal operating expenses, at the conclusion of a capital payment-pledge program; yet, as has been said, such a drive will bring a sizable increase in support —and that support will be sustained if there can be an opportunity for it to stabilize at that particular level over several years.

Maximum income from a parish will result if the cycle includes a capital-funds program at the outset that includes allowance for shortfall, a well-programmed Every-Member Canvass at the conclusion of the commitment-payment period, and a subsequent capital-funds program six years later.

In planning a ten-year ministry in a local church, a pastor would do well to conduct a good Every-Member Canvass the first year, a capital-funds program the second year, a comprehensive Every-Member Canvass in the fifth year, and a second capital-funds program in the tenth year. Since pastorates do not necessarily fall neatly into such a cycle, responsible parish leaders should consider adopting such a long-range plan, preferably to coincide with the beginning or ending of a pastor's ministry.

5

The Bid for Project Support

A PRESBYTERIAN ELDER and his wife made a gift of $27,500 to a hospital drive for an operating room. When asked why they had never done anything like this for their church the answer was, "No one has ever asked us." In every parish there are those who would contribute more in any one year than the total budget of the parish if they were so motivated.

In one parish a member's contribution to the annual church budget came to about $2,000 a year. Through the years the officers had considered this person off limits for special appeals on the ground that he was carrying more than his share of the load. Much of his philanthropy, as a result, went to hospitals, colleges, and so on. Actually, on one occasion he was approached for a special gift. The result was a block of securities totaling more in value than the total amount he had given to that parish in thirty-five years! This was repeated on three different occasions. His appreciation for the church and his zeal for its mission and outreach increased with each gift. He became one of the major contributors to the Fifty Million Fund of the United Presbyterian Church in the U.S.A. Had the four other appeals not been made, he would not have been so interested in the denominational effort.

Unfortunately, however, it is most difficult to raise sights for giving in this dimension for general support, be it an educational institution, health facility, or church. Large gifts must usually be paired with projects or program packages. This does not rule out the possibility of increased support for general administration and program if aspects of these are packaged for challenge giving. For example: Viewing a budget of $50,000 for a local church in its annual operation, it is difficult to appeal for a $10,000 gift. Donors generally view the total need, slice off a reasonable portion, and assume it as their proper share. This might well be in the area of $2,000. However, it is very possible to package the Christian Education Program in a prospectus for three years' support at $8,000 a year. The appeal then is for a gift of $24,000 to underwrite the program of Christian Education for three years. The prospectus must include something old, something new, something creative, and something unique to this experiment. Many will be surprised at the response to this approach from major contributors. The illustration in Christian Education could apply to Youth Work, Women's Work, Local and Regional Mission, Denominational Support, and Music Programs. In one congregation, one-half of a $500,000-appeal budget is underwritten by major contributors in project support defined in three-year packages.

The possibilities along this line are as boundless as the creativity of the imagination. One parish found itself constantly hampered by the limited number of persons who could play the piano or organ for services in the church, chapel, or events in connection with the Sunday school and devotional services in groups throughout the year. Sensing this need, a contributor made it possible for the church to employ a full-time minister of music. Included in his portfolio were twenty lessons in piano or organ each week, without charge, to members of the parish. The contract was funded and established for three years. After that the program was assumed by the parish budget. At the end of six years there were twelve persons in the parish who could play the organ for a Sunday morning service. Today five of those students are directors of music in churches of three denominations in that very city.

On another occasion it was important that a change be made in custodial service in a large plant. Qualified persons were almost impossible to employ. When the pastor spoke to the trustees about contracting maintenance service with a professional firm they thought it neither feasible or practical. When a commitment underwriting a contract for three years was in sight they acted favorably on the proposal, and since the three-year contract and commitment expired they have sustained the arrangement through an annual budget designation. The donor's support actually increased from $400 a year to $36,000 for a three-year period and released $24,000 of regularly budgeted funds for new program development.

Appeals of this type can be made at any time and need not necessarily be a part of the annual stewardship program structured in the fall. While the project is in a sense a part of the annual budget it must be presented as an opportunity for the parish to move beyond the limitations of ordinary budget procedures and enable the persons involved in the special commitment to share in the enthusiasm of a broader experience with the members of the parish whose program is enlarged and whose potential for mission is increased.

The appeal for project support is often most effective when a commitment is sought on a ten-quarter or thirty-month basis. It is almost startling in its freshness, yet it retains the advantage of providing funding in three annual budgets just as did the more traditional three-year package. Potential contributors who may feel overcommitted at the moment frequently welcome it as it enables them to move into project support at some specific time in the future. Most important of all, if such an appeal is made at the beginning of a year it enables a church to shift a significant part of its support away from the annual Every-Member Canvass, thus introducing a new element of flexibility into the financial and program life of the church. For these reasons, experience has proven the thirty-month package to be particularly attractive to those of affluence, and a positive addition to the financial structure of a church.

Local committees may consider project support from many points of view. Consider these illustrations:

• Two neighborhood churches were anxious to develop bell choirs. Neither had the hand bells required for such a program. One church had a sizable membership, but few members of affluence. The other congregation was quite small, but included in its membership several well-to-do persons. Both were successful in securing hand bells, and the dedication ceremonies were spaced only a few weeks apart. The first parish invited members to purchase a single bell as a memorial or gift. All twenty-five bells were purchased through individual gifts ranging in size from $20 to $78 each. The second parish announced the need, and a single contributor, requiring anonymity, provided the entire set.

• A congregation consisting largely of blue-collar workers had stretched itself to build an addition to the sanctuary for Sunday-school classrooms. At the dedication service there was an open house, and the first visitor was distressed to note that inadequate equipment would limit use of the facilities for some time. The most obvious need was for seating. He placed a chair on a table, made a poster with a red Magic Marker and appealed for persons to buy a chair for $9.50. When the open house was completed, funds had been contributed for sixty-four brand-new steel chairs. Here was a project that succeeded because of need and was developed spontaneously as one person envisioned a solution in which many would gladly share.

• A Midwestern United Church of Christ congregation arranged for the installation of a new pipe organ. The console and organ chamber capacity were larger than the installation required. The Organ Committee, with the recommendation of the trustees and approval of the congregation, programmed for the future with plans for the addition of one stop and one rank of pipes each year. The initial projection has been surpassed by fourteen gifts in eight years, increasing the size of the instrument by 30 percent. Eleven stops and ranks of pipes were given as memorials, with a brass plaque providing a permanent witness to those remembered. The other three were funded by members of the parish having particular zeal for instrumental music.

• A United Methodist church was anxious to build on the music program in the public schools. Envisioned were an orchestra, robed choirs, and improved equipment. They outlined basic needs and established projects in terms of books for instrumental music, uniforms, choir robes, and a vocal music library including certain instruments to loan, such as drums and a harp. The church now has four choirs, a bell choir, a band, and an orchestra. The church has also developed a unique program as a singing musical church drawing families from great distances. This church has survived neighborhood blight, community change, and racial imbalance. An expert program of music, based on project support, has increased a people's faith and zeal and helped a church survive.

When project support is under consideration, it is important to ask the question: Who makes the appeal? The answer to this question is crucial, yet in this area the church has much to learn. Because such support is almost always program related, it is most probable that the pastor, or senior pastor in a multiple staff situation, is the key person in its presentation and interpretation. Yet few there are indeed who are trained in this field. The observation has been made that the clergy have been taught everything in the seminary except how to run a church. Certainly most pastors know little about raising money and yet today this is an important function of the pastoral ministry in almost every parish.

In most organizations major appeals are made by, or under the signature of, the top permanent officer. This is not the Clerk of Session, President of the Board of Trustees or Chairman of the Board of Deacons or Vestry. The top officer in the parish is the pastor. He must make the appeal and/or be prominent in it.

The Stewardship Departments of our denominations would do well to bring pastors from every section of the country together for special training sessions in this field. Support for local churches, as well as denominational causes, would be greatly increased by doing this. Funds presently going to charitable causes when professionals are at work would have a run for their money if the denominations were to train pastors in the parish to provide leadership in this area.

Of course we need to realize that every pastor cannot be trained, or become fully qualified, in this field. Some just cannot do the job. Their gifts are in other areas equally important to the mission of the church.

In these situations, what alternatives are there to the pastor? Persons who deal in finance, who are not afraid of a reasonable challenge, and who are truly dedicated to the vision of the church will qualify.

The church is impoverished today because our sights are too low and our expertise underdeveloped for the development of adequate resources.

Project support is a means by which every church can articulate its mission for meaningful response among those who share the vision of a particular aspect of the Kingdom of God. Project resources may make the difference between success and failure in a local church budget in any one year.

6

Mail Solicitation

MAIL SOLICITATION is almost synonymous with financial development. Usually, however, we tend to think of such mail solicitations as related especially to organizations two steps away from the individual—that is, those organizations that raise millions of dollars a year through mail solicitation, but which do not seek to involve their donors personally and directly in a program or some form of service. The local church is one of the few institutions that is a single step from the individual. Few organizations have so keen and personal a relationship with the individual and the group.

As mail solicitation is important to second-step agencies, so is it important to the first-step agency as well. Any really adequate stewardship emphasis on the local level requires mail communication. The average Every-Member Canvass involves several mailings, including one announcing the overall plan, one presenting the proposed budget, and, when the effort is person-to-person in visitations, one that serves as a follow-up letter to those who could not be reached by the visitor.

How is mail solicitation related to the several areas of communication providing resources for mission?

• *First*, the mailing list. The average church has a mailing list and most are limited to the resident and nonresident membership. Some include in the list courtesy mailings involving denominational officials and other pastors and congregations with which exchange is made for ideas, experience, and experiments. Usually the mailing

51

list ends there. A mailing list in a local parish should be much broader than this. It should include all of the following:

—prospects for membership. Those persons and families who have visited services or shared in events of parish life.

—persons who are related to the church through family participation. They may have membership in another parish in the area, the city, or some distant place. A son may be in the Boy Scouts, a daughter in the Girl Scouts, the father a member of a bowling team or the mother involved in the Women's Association.

—executives of corporations in which members and friends of the parish are employed.

—business executives of companies located in and/or serving the parish area.

—political leaders who have concerns in the parish area.

—key officers and staff persons of agencies serving the city and parish area.

—alumni. They are most important. Those who were raised in the church and church school, those whose roots were deep in the parish program, those who have a strong sentimental relationship to the church although they have moved great distances away and presently hold membership in other parishes, in some cases even other denominations. Some may have been involved in the parish for only a short time while resident there.

—property owners and residents of the parish area whose property values are increased because the church is there.

—families the pastor or others have served when need for some form of ministry has arisen. A death occurred in the family, they had no church connection, the pastor was invited, perhaps through the funeral director, to conduct a memorial service. Or an accident occurred in which a family member was injured or disease made inroads into a family's life, and the parish responded with a chaplaincy function.

The mailing list should never be considered complete. Each week some names will be deleted and others included. It is a constant process. It should always be up to date and an adequate tool for reaching those to whom the local church should interpret parish need.

• *Second,* a newsletter. Each parish needs a communication piece. It may be weekly, monthly, or quarterly. The weekly publication tends to become too commonplace. It is difficult, in most parishes, to have a single event in each of fifty-two weeks that can truly challenge interest and stimulate valid response. The Sunday Order of Service is not generally newsworthy in and of itself. The quarterly publication is often too removed from a vital function. The monthly publication is, however, frequent enough to sustain identity and also represents a time segment in which a truly significant event can and should occur. If the publication is monthly, then two issues each year should be addressed to stewardship or financial development. This should be the subject of the entire issue, and everything should be written with the cause of stewardship uppermost in mind.

The quality of the publication is as important as its content. The mimeograph sheet is cheap and the response is usually pennies. But the church cannot operate on pennies, nickels, dimes, quarters, or even dollars. The movie theater on the corner will have a larger admission fee than any of these. Whenever possible, it is wise to secure expertise in the field either on a contract or volunteer basis. The tools and procedures of our askings must be consistent with the gift we seek.

In making such a decision it is important to consider true cost accounting. Often the best businessmen lose good business sense when they attend a church board meeting. One parish 'that had been using a mimeographed communication piece for many years was persuaded to make a careful cost accounting of the entire procedure in terms of staff time, equipment, materials, and postage. To the surprise of many it was discovered that there would be a saving in excess of 25 percent by turning to commercial letterpress for producing the newsletter. With inflation, and the development of cold type, offset and computer, it is likely that the percentage factor in economy would still prevail. Whether it does or it does not is not really the important issue. The issue is quality of presentation. If laundry soap, deodorants, and razor blades are entitled to an impressive posture, how much more so is the church and the mission of Christ to these times!

The content of the communication piece is as important as its quality and appearance. It should not be weighted with statistics nor endeavor to impress the reader with staff. A parish is in a tragic situation if its most important asset is its building and minister. Mission and service to people is the important function. People give to people! Those who will contribute to your parish are those who will be impressed with what you are doing with and for people. If the particular need at the moment is facility or building—then the message must center on the service these may provide to persons. Focus the content of your communication piece on the people who serve and the people who are served as a result of your gift. Elaborate on the service each gift makes possible.

This newsletter should be sent to all persons on the mailing list. As persons are added to the mailing list announce the fact to them in a personal letter. Give a brief description of the purpose of the publication and express the hope that they will be better informed of parish life and mission as a result of receiving it. Make clear that they are invited, through the publication, to participate in and support the parish.

When particular items are included in the publication that provide opportunity for response, the tool for response should be included. That is, the telephone number if it is a message, an envelope with commitment form if it is resources. The two issues addressed to stewardship and financial development should include both a form for response and a mailing envelope. Even if the desired response is for a person to bring a commitment form to a service, less than half may find it possible to attend. All should have adequate opportunity to respond, however, and the response procedure must be facilitated as much as possible.

The publication should have a peculiar identity easily recognized by the recipient. Yet the primary emphasis should be on eye catching, impressive and stimulating design. All parts of the mailing should be of equal quality. Economies in any part will prove damaging to the whole.

If the commitment form is a commitment of resources, it should be structured to provide options in response, namely, the immediate gift and programmed giving in terms of monthly, quarterly, semi-annual, or annual remittance. Do not overlook the possibility of thirty-month, ten-quarter or three-year commitment. The most desirable, of course, is the open-end commitment that will be sustained until revised or forbidden.

Among the various kinds of communications, none is of more importance than letters. These will be sent out on many occasions, for various reasons, and with varying rationales. But now we are particularly concerned with the fund-raising letter. Letters for fund raising should be simply stated and limited to one page, but comprehensive in providing information concerning the purpose, need, resources presently available, and a projection of costs to implement the program. Also included, of course, will be some description of benefits the resources will provide in meeting the needs of people.

Letters should be personally addressed, individually typed, and signed by either the person whose signature is used or someone empowered to sign the letters for the person sending them. The letters should go over the signature of a person of influence. In some cases it will be the pastor, a leading officer in the parish, or an outstanding lay person, respected and dedicated. No person's name should be used unless that person has already made a meaningful, significant commitment. Permission to use a name should never be enough. The appeal must be honest and it will not be honest unless it represents a valid commitment.

Often when the response is received it is assumed that the task is done. This is one of the gravest errors made in fund raising today. Each commitment must be acknowledged, again with a personally addressed, individually typed and signed letter. These letters fall into three categories: *First*, the letter addressed to those who sustain a commitment at the previous level of support. *Second*, the letter addressed to those who increase their support. Here, an expression of appreciation and a pledge to be worthy of trust is in order. *Third*, a letter to those who reduce support. This letter should express appreciation for previous support, the present commitment, and a statement that should personal service be desired in the event of problems or difficulty the organization stands ready to help.

In some unusual circumstances, when an appeal is directed for a cause of an emergency nature or a once-in-a-lifetime need, it is impressive to send a letter with multiple signatures. The desirable number is three. Two may be adequate, but four, or more, is too many. In this event the letters must be personally signed by the three persons or those authorized to use their signature on the letters. Even if authorized, one person should not sign all three names. Here, again, the persons sharing in the program appeal must be thoroughly dedicated. Without a firm, valid commitment the effort will be meaningless.

What are the prospects for support from those suggested to be included on the mailing list?

• *Prospects for membership.* Many people will not join a church, for all sorts of reasons. They may believe they will be in the area for only a short time, have strong ties to a previous congregation or have reservations about membership in a particular parish. Nevertheless, they can provide sizable support in every parish. Certainly not all, but a significant percentage of them will give.

• *Persons who are related to the church through family participation.* The appeal to them is often as meaningful as to parish members themselves. They sense an obligation for opportunities the parish provides to their families. Large support can come from this group. On some occasions the largest contribution has come from this sector.

• *Executives of corporations and business executives.* The corporate sector supports many worthy causes. Business firms generally have been generous in their response. Usually, however, their response has been greater toward particular projects than for ongoing programs.

• *Political leaders who have a concern in the parish area.* Usually their gift is of a token nature. Yet they, too, welcome the opportunity to be involved.

• *Agency officers and staff persons.* Often the resources they can provide are other than financial. Mail reaching their desk from your parish may provide your church with an opportunity to occupy a significant role in community service, for many times they will approach you for participation in facets of programming through facilities or people that will expand the mission of the local church.

• *Alumni.* Colleges, universities, seminaries, and prep schools turn to their alumni for assistance throughout the years. Seldom does the local church think of its alumni. While pastor in Warsaw I invited the Reverend Dr. Richard Paul Graebel of the Springfield First Presbyterian Church to conduct a preaching mission. He wanted to know why I had invited him. My answer: "We are a feeder church. Our young people leave the community for higher education and never return. Three of our alumni are officers in your church. I want my people to learn the connection between our local church and the broader mission."

For some, the primary years in church experience are the most meaningful years of their life. They come to appreciate the role of the feeder church if they are a product of the same, and then, being knowledgeable of the feeder-church role, they will share substantially to assist the hometown church in its important mission.

In the mobile society, church members are on the move. They may relate to a particular church for only a few years. Some unique experience while a member of that particular parish may, however, cause them to think of this relationship as the high point in their spiritual life. Appreciation for that peculiar mission will cause them to share with zeal, because their gifts may enable that church to provide like instrumentality for others in the future.

There are dozens of reasons why alumni can be interested and are willing to share. This does not mean that the local church competes with the current affiliation. The intent should be supportive of present membership. But there is support potential above and beyond that for which a church can lay its claim, and unless this potential is claimed by the former church it is usually lost for Christian witness.

- *Property owners and residents of the parish community.* Here, usually, support is greatest when projects involve the physical properties of the church. Those things that prove to be an asset to the community will often be funded substantially by them.

- *Families to whom the particular ministry of the church has been given.* These, through the years, are the strongest prospects for membership and financial support. Though not united with the church, they will usually want to express gratitude for ministry through the sharing of resources not only once but time and time again.

Mail solicitation is more than solicitation. Actually it is communication. It is the means by which we communicate with the constituency our purpose and mission and the means by which that constituency may respond. The broader the base of understanding, the greater the response is certain to be.

7

Grants

GRANTSMANSHIP is an increasingly important field in financial development for the local church. Colleges and universities, hospitals and clinics, institutions and organizations have utilized grantsmanship especially from governmental agencies. Dormitories, field houses, and other educational facilities on campuses have been funded largely through government grants. While institutions and organizations have long utilized this funding source, local churches that have taken advantage of these opportunities are few and far between. Some do an exceptionally good job in developing projects and programs that qualify for this type of support. But most leaders in the church—especially at the level of the local church—are not familiar with either the opportunities or the procedures of grantsmanship.

Yet across the country there are a great number of hospitals that have been developed by denominations and in some cases by local churches. Homes for the aged, low- and middle-income housing, day-care centers, rehabilitation centers, training facilities, and dozens of other pressing opportunities and needs are met by the charitable organizations. Statutes and laws are designed with them in mind.

But government is not the total picture. Grantsmanship is illustrated by a parish that received into its membership a staff member of the American Red Cross. She was especially interested in developing an experimental program among the aged that would assist them in their life-style as they became more aged and yet help them keep the independence of living in their own homes. She needed space and she needed people. The church had both. She approached the pastor of the church, sharing her concern, the need, and the opportunity she believed this project would provide to the local church in service and in mission, and, in a sense, in financial subsidy as well. The proposition was presented to the officers. It gained their approval, and the pilot project was carried out through that local Presbyterian church. This was most unusual in that the project, grant, and granting procedure were implemented by the American Red Cross and not by the local church. This was the reverse of the ordinary procedure.

Similar steps were taken by another parish when the Association for Help to Retarded Children (AHRC) needed facilities, volunteer assistance, and equipment, which the local church had. The utilization of space, equipment, and people made for economy in the parish's program, provided a service to the community, and in the end brought new resources to their institution. This, too, was a process in reverse. Implementation came from the organization rather than the local church.

The converse is true in the First United Church in Fairbanks, Alaska. This church stands head and shoulders above all the parishes I have visited in our fifty states in utilizing grantsmanship to the fullest extent possible in a relatively small church out of the mainstream of urban life, with limited facilities and leadership. Yet, on a recent visit I saw their day-care center, facilities for training secretaries, office managers, key-punch operators, and classes for mentally retarded and emotionally disturbed children. Here were vocational training and rehabilitation. All with government funds! All using every square foot of floor space in the educational wing and basement. All enhancing the mission of the church. All assisting in part in underwriting the cost of maintaining the building, providing custodial services, and providing for adequate administrative staff and facilities to sustain this broad ministry of reconciliation.

Riverside Church in New York City provides many services to the Morningside Heights community. Among them is the day-care center for children. The service is provided each working day, and the eighteen-month-old baby receives excellent care while her mother works. Diapers are provided through the program as well as food and other needs. The cost, to the mother, is $2.60 per week based on a formula of earned income and rent. Gladstone L. Chandler, the Administrative Officer who serves as business manager at that church, reports that they receive about a quarter of a million dollars a year in grants to cover the cost of this one program. Certainly it is a part of the mission of the church. Actually it is made possible through funding from Federal and local sources.

Dozens of other illustrations—meals on wheels, family planning, alcohol and drugs—some not as large, all equally significant, could be marshaled to further emphasize that grants resources from foundations, corporations, organizations, and governmental agencies are available to assist the church in mission.

How do we go about securing grants for mission in the local church?

• Let us begin with government. Each church should have in its library the catalogue of *Federal and Domestic Assistance* published by the United States Government and available from the Government Printing Office, Washington, D.C., 20503. The original volume has several supplements each year and these are included in the initial subscription price. There are literally thousands of funding sources provided in this invaluable tool. Several paragraphs are devoted to each funding source defining the program, budget, number of grants, and size of the grants. Provided also is a listing of the types of organizations eligible for grants. In addition the name and address of the funding agency, the person to whom correspondence should be addressed, and the procedure to be followed in applying for a grant are given. As you leaf through this book you will be impressed not only by the scope of concern but also by the eligibility of the local church to share in exciting and new dimensions of ministry that will certainly enhance mission.

Many organizations and institutions qualify for grants from a particular agency and certainly most agencies receive more applications than they can fund. Because of the volume of applications received, yours must be exceptional; and if it is to be funded you must secure the name of, and make direct contact with, the person responsible for your application.

Three weeks after you have filed an application, review the application carefully for errors or any place where a revision could be helpful. Having done so, address a letter to the agency indicating the change or changes to be made in the application, providing both chapter and verse inasmuch as the application forms often consist of twenty to twenty-five pages. As a result of this letter you will receive a letter from the person in the agency who is responsible for your application, informing you that the changes are being made. When you receive this letter you have jumped a most important hurdle in the eventual funding of your grant. The proposal will not be funded if it does not become exceptional and if you, as an applicant, do not discover the contact name and develop the person-to-person relationship most important to approval and funding. When you have the name of the person in the agency responsible for your application, you can proceed to set up appointments in which you can receive his or her counsel and incorporate these suggestions in further revisions in your application and program. As the agency person becomes involved in the project the tendency will be for him or her to develop a greater zeal for it and the likelihood of funding will correspondingly increase.

Government grants usually require four to six months for implementation and the grant period may extend into several years. Funding is available from agencies in the Federal, state, county and municipal governments. In some cases one will be complementing another. In other cases the project will be related uniquely to one level of government and a single agency.

• A second area of funding resources is that of private foundations. The Foundation Center, 888 Seventh Avenue, New York, N.Y., 10106, publishes three volumes that are most important in this field. First, *The Foundation Directory*. The ninth edition of this invaluable compendium came from the press in May 1983. Second, *The Foundations Grants Index*, 12th Edition. Here in various categories are listed the grants made by the large foundations in the recent period. Third, the *National Data Book*, the Seventh Edition. Some twenty thousand funding sources are listed in the first and third volumes suggested above. Yet, these are only the tip of the iceberg. The National Consultation on Financial Development has access to some fifty thousand funding sources in the United States, and a local church, as a nonprofit organization, is eligible for service. The cost is modest and the service of matching proposals with the ten most likely funding sources among those

DISTRIBUTION OF FOUNDATION GRANTS, 1983

Field	Grants	Dollar Value	% of Grants
Welfare	10,960	$509,202,800	34.1
Education	5,775	286,005,941	17.9
Health	5,347	389,520,571	16.6
Cultural Activities	5,151	277,306,737	16.0
Social Science	2,225	132,062,310	6.9
Science	2,043	160,917,379	6.4
Religion	664	37,503,575	2.1

Source: 465 of the largest foundations as reported in the *Foundations Grants Index*, 13th Edition.

fifty thousand agencies and foundations is unique among services provided in this field. A local or regional ecumenical agency could facilitate participation in the National Consultation on Financial Development's services by orchestrating searches on a per diem basis. Information can be secured from their national offices at 31 Langerfeld Road, Hillsdale, N.J., 07642 (201 664-8890).

It is difficult to match projects with funding sources and the expertise is expensive. For example, an independent research specialist has a fee of $130 an hour. He cannot guarantee that he will successfully match a project with a potential resource even on a ten-hour contract basis. He will try, but the organization must carry the risk. His research may provide thirty potential resource services. When proposals are mailed, 3 percent response in initial interest may be expected from funding sources. When negotiations begin for foundation grants, the project usually is six to eighteen months from funding, with twelve months probably representing a reasonable average.

Again, it is important to develop personal contacts with funding sources. Appointments are difficult to arrange. The person from out of town is likely to be given priority for appointments. Those readily accessible because they are close at hand usually are put off until some other time and that some other time is usually a time that does not come.

In preparing the proposal it is important to know that procedures have changed drastically in the last decade. Previously it was important to prepare an impressive document, provide as much information as possible and include supporting documents in terms of constitution and bylaws, officers of the sponsoring institution, and biographies of those responsible for the project. Usually the audited financial report from the previous full fiscal year was included as well. When one wrote a foundation proposal he actually wrote a book. This is becoming less and less necessary or desirable. Today an initial proposal, if possible, should be under three pages in length. It should include a brief description of the project, needs, and purpose; and it should point up the positive benefits that are likely to ensue as a result of this initial funding grant. Included, as well, should be budget projections, a timetable, and indices for progress reports during the program. These will provide enough information for the foundation executive to know whether or not this is a project that will be of interest to the board of directors. If it is of interest, he will respond with a request for further information, perhaps arrange an interview with those responsible for the program, and request other supporting documents deemed desirable to the foundation for their files and report procedures.

Here is a procedure I like to use in connection with foundation proposals:

First, I send a letter to the foundation director indicating that a proposal will be sent to him at an early date. The letter includes the name of the proposal, the purpose of the project, and the person over whose signature the proposal will be sent.

Second, a letter including the proposal is sent to the foundation director, bearing the signature of the person responsible for the project or under whose supervision the project will be carried out.

Third, I send a follow-up letter indicating that the proposal has been sent and that I am prepared to meet with the foundation staff to discuss the proposal further, to answer questions and provide further documentation that may be desirable. In some cases an appointment follows. In other cases a letter response indicates that the material presented to this date is adequate for their consideration or else notification is given that the project does not fall in line with priorities established by the foundation at that particular moment.

Keep in mind that just because a foundation responds negatively

SAMPLE APPLICATION FOR FOUNDATION GRANT

EQUIPMENT FOR KAHULUI PRE-SCHOOL

Purpose: To secure capital funding for the newly established Kahului Union Pre-School, located in a key area on the Island of Maui, where services have been greatly under-developed and are urgently needed.

Description: Kahului is the key metropolitan area on the Island of Maui inasmuch as the principal air and shipping terminals form the hub for the economic life of the residents.

For the past several years families in the area have required the gainful employment of both spouses to make ends meet. The number now approaches seventy-five percent of those families with two parents. But at the same time there has been a sizeable increase in the single-parent families requiring preschool care for children while mothers are employed as the sole supporter of the family.

While every preschool, day-care, and nursery facility on the Island of Maui has continually had waiting lists, the situation in Kahului became critical for two reasons: First, facilities and services have been less than adequate for more than five years. Second, the Creative Nursery, which met the needs of seventy-five small children for many years closed, with the retirement of the Director in June 1984, leaving a great void in services to families in the Greater Kahului Area.

The pressing need for preschool child care on Maui, and especially in the Kahului Area, had been a deep concern of the Long Range Planning Committee of the Kahului Union Church. As a result, a special task force was established to study the need and the means whereby the Church could respond to meeting the need. This task force has been working with the Long Range Planning Committee since 1980, and the Executive Council presented the need for the Kahului Union Pre-School to the congregation for their concurrence. The three have made a commitment of the free use of facilities during the initial stage of operation and the service to be under the auspices of the Kahului Union Church during the organizational period, after which time it will become separately incorporated.

The Kahului Union Church is determined:

First, that the need of families who have preschool children be met.

Second, that mothers forced into full-time employment to provide, or supplement, family incomes may have access to qualified preschool care for dependent children.

Third, that the preschool provide quality child care with disciplines in personal and social relationships, moral and ethical values.

The Kahului Union Pre-School opened with service to two sections consisting of twenty-four children each in September 1984. Fees up to $135 per month have been assessed for children in Section I and $155 per month for those in Section II. A flexible schedule has been established that the preschool child care needs of deserving people are met.

The facilities used in the Kahului Union Church, while more than adequate, are twenty-five years old, and capital improvements of approximately twenty-five thousand dollars have been needed. These were identified as follows:

1. Increasing the height of the fence in the playground area for security reasons.
2. Placing a chain-link fence in the foreground that doors could be opened even when unattended.
3. Replacing old wooden slide doors with swinging doors with jalousies.
4. Replacing old windows with jalousie windows.
5. Renovating the kitchen for good services.
6. Installing ceiling fans to improve ventilation on hot windless days.
7. Replacing inadequate toilet facilities.
8. Installing cabinets to maximize multi-use of the facilities for evening and weekend projects and programs.
9. Replacing carpeting and repainting the entire facilities where preschool children are cared.
10. Installing chalk boards and bulletin boards.

An additional fourteen thousand dollars was required for administration, classroom, teaching, and food service needs ranging from cooking utensils to tape recorders, construction paper to playground equipment. Approximately ten thousand dollars was estimated to be spent on equipment that would meet the long-term needs of the preschool and an additional four thousand dollars in inventories to be sustained by tuitions and fees.

Limited funding was advanced from restricted funds by the Kahului Union Church to establish the Kahului Union Pre-School, as loans. Gifts of cash and equipment have been received from donors and four grants totaling the sum of $8,000 from foundations. The Kahului Union Pre-School opened with essential modifications met on September 1, 1984. Funding must be secured to complete the work and acquire the necessary equipment.

While it is important that funding from community sources be secured as soon as possible, the budget processes for grants from foundations and corporations will be respected and gratefully received in the time frame essential to the funding source's grant procedures.

Budget:	1984-85 including capital funding needs.	
	Salaries for staff and substitutes	$ 48,770.80
	Medical and unemployment insurance, Workman's Compensation, and FICA	13,804.92
	Administration	2,223.84
	Capital needs (Items 1-10)	25,000.00
	Materials and supplies for teaching and child care	14,880.00
	Rent (Contributed by Kahului Union Church) with utilities	30,000.00
	Total	$134,679.56
	Receipts:	
	Tuitions and fees	$ 62,640.00
	Rent and utilities (Kahului Union Church)	30,000.00
	Grants	39,070.00
	Other	2,969.56
	Total	$134,679.56

Funding Need: $19,070

Chairman: William Kinaka
Kahului Union Pre-School Task Force
Post Office Box 574
Kahului, Hawaii 96732
(808) 871-4422

This proposal was written by the author. It was submitted to ten foundations selected by the National Consultation on Financial Development. Five foundations made grants toward this funding need.

to a particular proposal at the moment does not mean that this will necessarily be the policy of the foundation at a later date. Proposals turned down at one time may be approved for funding ten months later. This has been particularly true in the field of ecology. Foundations not conscious of environmental needs at one particular moment in the ecological revolution became alert and broadened their policy to include grants for such projects in a comparatively short period of time. Similarly, President Richard Nixon's visit to Peking, as another example, did much to revolutionize West-East attitudes overnight. As a result, funding policies in many foundations reversed immediately.

If the response is negative, be guided by the nature of the response in taking further action. When the foundation indicates that all funds in the particular field have been allocated, remember that there may be opportunity in the next fiscal year. When the foundation responds that the proposal is not in the area of their priorities at the present time, watch for reports that will indicate their priorities have changed. When the foundation suggests a particular source of funding as a possibility, be sure to follow through on the recommendation. Some of the best leads to funding come from foundation executives who are sympathetic to the program and have connections that are helpful in discovering valid funding sources.

• Grants are made by corporations to deserving projects and programs. Not long ago the executive of a Midwest ecumenical organization responded negatively to the suggestion of corporate support. He stated that there were no corporate funds in his area available for such a religious organization. The chairman of the Finance Committee was quick to mention that the air-conditioning unit for the executive offices had been a gift from a corporation. The need had been known to a corporate executive and his board of directors had responded affirmatively. There was no formal written proposal. However, the need and knowledge of the purpose of such a gift and its value to the program of the organization resulted in a grant. This is grantsmanship in the best sense of the word.

• Organizations, too, are sources for grants. At the beginning of this chapter a project funded by the American Red Cross was described. In many cases it will involve the merging of program and mission, the sharing of facilities and staff, the utilization of common properties for the common good. Literally dozens of organizations come to mind as we consider program development in the local church. When the mission of the church is to people, almost every organization structured to meet particular needs in society becomes a possible source for grants and/or expanded program. In one church more than thirty organizations share in facets of programming that require two hundred and seventeen scheduled meetings each month!

Learning to think in terms of foundation support may well introduce some unexpected benefits into the life of a congregation. For regardless of whether we look for program resources to government, foundation, corporation, and organization or agency, we will almost certainly discover that we must plan the program in such a way that it will not be limited to our particular membership or our particular race of people, although a minority group may well be an exception at this juncture. Basically, however, the effort must be intercultural, interracial, and ecumenical. It is a sad situation when a local church's mission does not qualify on all three counts.

Moreover, as you view the spectrum for program development on the local level you will often find that the dimensions really possible are beyond the capability of a particular parish. Here it is well to consider the mission of the church in a larger dimension than that of the local parish. Here is a challenge to learn to think in terms of the total community, the entire city or area. As you discover needs, opportunities, and the role of the church in these times you may well discover that the work that can best be done will be done only as one particular parish joins in concert with another parish or parishes to meet the need. Here is an opportunity for the utilization of staff, facilities, equipment, and expertise that will be greater than that available from any single group and at the same time will qualify for greater mission in the service of Christ and His church.

Learning to think in terms of foundation support will have the advantage of teaching us to think in terms of local resources. Too often when we think of foundations we think of the large foundations. In a recent meeting with the executives of the United Methodist Foundation in New Mexico I was told that.there were only five foundations in that state. When I returned to my office and explored comprehensive listings I discovered literally dozens of resources not known to them.

Similarly, when we think of corporations we tend to think of the corporate giants. Most companies, even those privately owned, share their resources. Resources for youth programming, projects for the aged, facilities and materials for children, the physically handicapped, the mentally retarded, and the emotionally disturbed are actually almost unlimited. The greatest limitation is in our hesitancy or failure to make needs known. Contributions budgets are based upon earnings. Whether you invite their support or not, the allocated funds will be distributed. Your invitation may make funds otherwise unavailable to Christian mission a resource for your local church.

Grants provide newfound resources for program and project support in the local church. Federal domestic assistance, state and local governments, corporations, foundations, fraternal bodies and nonprofit organizations all have program ideas that may be implemented through the local church. As congregations view mission in terms of community, and not parish, the church becomes a contemporary institution in the age to which it ministers.

8

The Gift Annuity

THE GIFT ANNUITY PLAN has long been a fundamental part of the financial support of schools, hospitals, and other institutions and deserves to be explored more fully by the local church. It is a plan by which individuals invest funds with the local church and frequently increase their income and gain distinct tax benefits even while their investment is working to strengthen the church's life and mission. Here is a simple case illustration:

An 82-year-old communicant presents securities having a market value of $10,000 to his church. (The presentation may be made to a local, regional, or national ecumenical organization, denomination, institution, or agency.) In return, the communicant receives an annual income of $1,020 a year for as long as he lives. Payments can be made monthly, quarterly, semiannually, or annually. Of this $1,020 a year only $248 is taxable income. Previously, his income from the securities was about $425 a year and the entire amount was taxable. Through a Gift Annuity he has doubled his annual income from the $10,000 investment without increasing his tax load. Actually, he has a 75 percent exclusion from taxes on his increased annual income. The program is possible as a result of a provision in the Internal Revenue Code designed to assist funding in religious and charitable organizations.

The benefits described so far, however, are only part of the story. The total benefits for tax purposes are far greater than the tax exclusion on annual income. In the particular case under discussion there are two additional benefits. First, the gift value of this particular contract is approximately $4,899. This may be applied for credit as a contribution in the year that the contract is written or carried over as many as five succeeding years if appropriate to the donor. In the event that it is spread over six years—that is, the year in which it is written and the five succeeding years—the amount to be claimed as a contribution each year may vary from year to year. This will be determined by the donor and his financial counsel, to provide the greatest advantage possible in the light of his total tax situation.

A second benefit is that, as in this case, the agreement was negotiated through the transfer of appreciated securities to the charitable organization. Because this was the case, the value of the securities as measured against the actuarial value of the agreement is $2,982. By transferring the securities to the charitable organization the donor has realized capital gains on only $2,119!

Experience has shown that persons entering Gift Annuity Agreements with charitable organizations through appreciated securities will frequently have the full value of their investment returned to them in three years, when all factors are considered: the rate of annual return, the tax exclusion on the annual income, the gift value determined at the time the contract is written, and the capital-gain advantage obtained because any gain is figured against the actuarial value rather than the face value of the contract.

Here, in brief, are the advantages in the space of three years under this contract:

Gift value $4,899; Growth not subject to capital gain $4,899; Return over three years $3,060; Three-year exclusion on annual income $2,295; Benefits accrue to $15,154.

The actual value of each of these benefits for any specific individual must be determined by an accountant on the basis of the 1040 Income Tax Form. The following schedule will be helpful in ascertaining benefits as far as annual return and tax exclusion on annual return are concerned.

In addition to these benefits to the donor, such a contract provides a very real benefit for a local church. The exact amount will depend upon how the annuity is handled by the local church. There are several ways in which this may be done:

SINGLE LIFE CHARITABLE GIFT ANNUITIES

Approximate Benefits per $1,000.00, based on quarterly payments*

Age**	Annual % rate	Annual amount	For men			For women		
			Taxable per year	Gift value	Actuarial value	Taxable per year	Gift value	Actuarial value
60	7.0	70.00	25.27	189.61	810.39	29.47	123.39	876.61
61	7.0	70.00	24.50	207.39	792.61	28.84	139.21	860.79
62	7.1	71.00	24.28	214.67	785.33	28.61	143.46	856.54
63	7.1	71.00	23.43	233.70	766.30	27.97	160.50	839.50
64	7.2	72.00	23.18	242.70	757.30	27.72	166.46	833.54
65	7.3	73.00	22.85	252.70	747.30	27.37	173.42	826.58
66	7.4	74.00	24.57	263.77	736.23	27.01	181.49	818.51
67	7.5	75.00	22.20	275.87	724.13	26.85	190.52	809.48
68	7.6	76.00	21.74	288.87	711.13	26.37	200.63	799.37
69	7.7	77.00	21.25	302.92	697.08	26.18	211.75	788.25
70	7.8	78.00	21.22	317.89	682.11	25.97	223.98	776.02
71	7.9	79.00	21.09	333.71	666.29	25.67	237.25	762.75
72	8.0	80.00	20.40	350.40	649.60	25.36	251.44	748.56
73	8.2	82.00	20.50	360.15	639.85	25.34	257.65	742.35

74	8.3	83.00	20.92	378.66	621.34	24.98	274.16	725.84
75	8.5	85.00	20.91	390.80	609.20	25.33	283.11	716.89
76	8.7	87.00	20.79	404.14	595.86	25.58	293.56	706.44
77	8.9	89.00	21.45	418.65	581.35	25.36	305.53	694.47
78	9.1	91.00	22.02	434.25	565.75	25.57	318.77	681.23
79	9.4	94.00	21.90	444.84	555.16	26.70	326.30	673.70
80	9.6	96.00	23.42	462.50	537.50	26.88	342.50	657.50
81	9.9	99.00	24.16	475.60	524.40	27.22	353.33	646.67
82	10.2	102.00	24.79	489.90	510.10	28.36	365.87	634.13
83	10.6	106.00	25.55	500.63	499.37	29.68	373.96	626.04
84	10.9	109.00	27.25	517.24	482.76	29.76	389.71	610.29
85	11.4	114.00	29.41	526.22	473.78	32.49	396.14	603.86
86	11.8	118.00	31.39	540.74	459.26	33.75	409.88	590.12
87	12.3	123.00	33.58	552.53	447.47	35.30	420.55	579.45
88	12.8	128.00	35.58	565.31	434.69	36.61	433.09	566.91
89	13.4	134.00	37.65	575.76	424.24	39.66	443.10	556.90
90	14.0	140.00	39.34	586.86	413.14	42.70	455.12	544.88

*All rates are from May 1983 Conference on Gift Annuities.
**In determining age, figure from nearest birthday.
Tables computed by Raymond B. Knudsen II.

• *First*, the contract may be negotiated through the denominational foundation. And virtually all the major denominations have established such foundations. In this event the funds will probably be held by the foundation until the demise of the annuitant. At that time the residual funds—there may be gains through appreciation or there may be losses in the event that operating expenses have been larger than earnings—are distributed to the local church. This method provides no immediate funding. This is definitely deferred giving.

• *Second*, at least in theory, the annuity agreement may be reinsured by the church or nonprofit organization through an annuity contract with an insurance company. The cost, in the case illustrated, would run in the neighborhood of $6,000. The remainder, or $4,000, would be immediately available to the local church. Unless the insurance policy is written with a shared risk by the local church, there would be no residual benefit. When risk is shared, the initial cost of the contract is greater and less would be available for use in the local church at the time the contract is written.

• *Third*, the annuity agreement may be reinsured through the National Consultation on Financial Development. This is a unique service and it deserves the widest explanation. Through a group insurance program the agency is able to negotiate the contract, issue the certificate, and make the annuity payments to the donor throughout the remainder of his or her life with unusually attractive terms. The rates presently in effect make possible the insuring of the annual income at a cost of $6,000. The agency charges an hourly fee and you may contract for its services. In the case illustrated, the local church would have $4,000 available immediately, at the time the contract is written.

In the light of all the factors, it is probably not wise for the local church to reinsure the contract with an underwriter or to manage an annuity independently. In many states statutes prohibit religious and charitable organizations from such procedures; and where it is possible the statutes on investment procedures are so rigid, the auditing procedures so minute and demanding, that it is not feasible or practical for the organization to undertake the task. When reinsuring the contract with an insurance company the policy income is to the church. The receiving of funds from the company and, in turn, the payment of income to the annuitant, or donor, is costly, time-consuming and a real nuisance. And in some cases regrets have been expressed by annuitants whose accounts have not been serviced properly. So far as the donor is concerned, the purpose of an annuity is to insure income and minimize anxieties and concerns. Unless the annuity is handled by experts who are able to use time-proven procedures, the organization will do a disservice to the annuitant by structuring a contract it is unable to service satisfactorily.

Unless a parish is large enough to generate a dollar volume of not less than $250,000 a year, and can be expertly staffed, it should not form its own investment proceedings for the Gift Annuity Program. Few parishes of any size can justify undertaking an operation that can be done more efficiently and effectively by their denomination or by the National Consultation on Financial Development in their behalf.

The shrinking tax umbrella may one day make significant changes in this kind of program, but in the eighties the Gift Annuity Program is one of the brightest stars on the horizon of opportunity in financial development.

There are several steps to be taken by an organization intending to establish a Gift Annuity Program:

• The governing board of the organization must become familiar with the program, adopt a policy for participation in the program, and implement procedures for informing members and friends of the unique opportunities provided through the Gift Annuity Plan.

• A local church should explore the opportunities provided by the denomination in serving the local parish through Gift Annuity Agreements. In some cases the denomination itself will have a foundation structured to service such contracts. In other cases this service may be provided by one or more of the boards and agencies of the denomination.

• When denominational structures are not available for a particular church or do not have a program providing immediate resources, it is possible to correspond with the National Consultation on Financial Development, 31 Langerfeld Road, Hillsdale, N.J., 07642 (201/664-8890). A local church is eligible for this service

(Name of Church or Agency)   (Mailing Address)

APPLICATION FOR A GIFT ANNUITY AGREEMENT

I/We hereby make application for:

_____ A Charitable Gift Annuity Agreement (payments begin within one year).

_____ A Deferred Payment Gift Annuity Agreement (payments deferred at least one year); the first payment to be made on _____ _____, _____.

               Month   Day   Year

I/We desire to give irrevocably to _____ (Church/Agency) on the gift annuity plan checked above the sum of $_____, and/or the securities or other assets listed here (use back of sheet if necessary):

ONE LIFE / TWO LIVES

Payments are to be made to: _____

( ) Male, ( ) Female.   (Print name in full—if Mrs., give own and husband's given names)

Address: _____

      (Street)   (City)   (State)   (Zip)

Date of birth:_____ Social Security Number:_____

Place of birth: _____

      (City)   (County)   (State)

> The following is to be filled out
> ONLY when a survivorship contract is desired.
>
> The Second Person: _____( ) Male, ( ) Female,   (Print name in full—if Mrs., give own and husband's given names)
>
> Address: _____
>   (Street)   (City)   (State)   (Zip)
>
> Date of birth: _____ Social Security Number: _____
> Place of birth: _____
>   (City)   (County)   (State)

I/We understand this gift will be used to benefit the purposes of (name of church or agency) as the governing board shall in its wisdom direct.

Signature of donor: _____

Social Security Number, if other than above: _____

Address: _____

      (Street)   (City)   (State)   (Zip)

Date of Application: _____
Signature of second person (if any) _____
Social Security Number: _____
Address: _____
     (Street)   (City)   (State)   (Zip)
Date of Application: _____

Please send this form, the check or securities covering the agreement, and proof of age, to:

YOUR CHURCH/AGENCY
ADDRESS
CITY/STATE/ZIP
PHONE

---

even if it does not contract for services with the agency. Such agreements also may be written through the agency for a local or regional ecumenical agency, a church related institution, a denomination, or almost any nonprofit religious or charitable organization.

• Explore several opportunities. There will be options in each. No one will require exclusive programming for all agreements. In some cases there will be advantages in utilizing the denominational structure. In some cases there will be advantages in utilizing the ecumenical structure. They are not in competition with each other. They seek to complement each other in their service to Christ and His Kingdom.

When a decision has been reached as to the procedures most desirable for the particular church or organization, it is then time to begin a program of information and interpretation. Some basic printed materials will be available from the denomination, agency, or organization through which the agreements will be processed. Supplementary materials can be prepared by the local group. The National Consultation on Financial Development, 31 Langerfeld Road, Hillsdale, N.J., 07642, has done excellent work along this line. In each case, materials prepared by the local group should be reviewed by legal counsel as well as by the organization, denomination, or agency through which the agreements will be processed.

Gift Annuities are most attractive to the 65-year-old and older group. Program a series of meetings and circulate literature especially prepared for them. Emphasis should be laid on the security of the investment, the income, the tax shelter, and the fact that the investment will expand the mission of the church in these times. Annuitants will have the pleasure of seeing their investment work for the Lord while they live.

A special committee consisting of persons knowledgeable about investments and insurance should be named on the local level to follow up the meetings and distribution of literature in order to answer any questions that may arise in the minds of prospects. The First Baptist Church of Cleveland has appointed such a Task Force with responsibility to answer questions and follow up on prospect leads. Three attorneys provide expertise to this enterprise.

In September of 1972 the Internal Revenue Service announced a revision in the Internal Revenue Code to provide opportunity for religious and charitable organizations to issue annuity contracts on a deferred-income basis. This has created an entirely new climate for investment income and annuity prospects. Until this revision was announced, the Gift Annuity Program was generally not a good investment for anyone in the forty-years-of-age bracket, regardless of the fringe benefits it offered. On the deferred-income basis, however, an individual in life's prime may enter an agreement with income to begin at age sixty-five. In the deferred-income plan the annuitant can command income return in retirement as high as 15 percent a year. Generally, however, a somewhat more conservative annual return based on present age and actuarials may be in store. This assures the individual of a quite attractive retirement income and is modest enough in demand to be reasonably reinsured by the organization so as to provide good resources for income on the deferred-income basis. This is a new opportunity for religious and charitable organizations, and very little literature is available for interpreting it at this time. However, as leaders become aware of the opportunity more consideration will be given to it.

As annuity agreements are negotiated on the local level they will increase in popularity. Few people in annuity programs have only one contract. One United Presbyterian annuitant has more than thirty contract agreements. Most annuitants related to church agencies have several. Once one agreement has been consummated there will be opportunity for subsequent agreements in the future.

In gratitude to God and confirming my/
our Christian Witness, I/We wish to make
a capital gift to First Baptist Church.

Please provide me/us with additional
information about:

___ The Gift Annuity. Amount $_____.
My age: _____. If for two life
agreement, age: _____, sex: _____ of
second person.

___ Deferred Payment Gift Annuity.
Amount $_____. Date you wish
payments to you to start: _____.
Age: _____. If for two life agreement,
age: _____, sex: _____ of second person.

___ Charitable Remainder Trusts.

___ Life Insurance.

___ Gift of Real Estate.

___ Wills and Bequests.

___ Gifts of Securities.

___ I/We wish to talk with the Minister
and/or a church officer.

___ Enclosed is my/our gift of _____ as
a gift to the ministry and mission of
First Baptist Church of Greater
Cleveland.

Name:_____

Address:_____

City/State/Zip:_____

Telephone:_____

**The First Baptist Church
of Greater Cleveland**
3630 Fairmount Boulevard
Cleveland, Ohio 44118
(216) 932-7480

The 6-page folded brochure shown on the next two pages has been
quite effective in raising funds for Churches.

The
First Baptist Church
of
Greater Cleveland

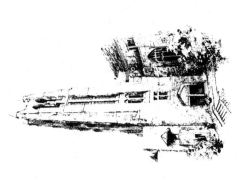

A DESIGN FOR
INTENTIONAL GIVING

THE GOSPEL IS THE GOOD NEWS OF SHARING

"God gave . . ."

Divine love is discerned in the fact that God gave. From the moment of the incarnation on, giving has been an integral part of the Christian life.

In Western Civilization, the support of humanitarian services, as well as the support of the churches, has been encouraged by government. In the United States, the Internal Revenue Code is devised to recognize the exercise of philanthropic giving.

Many of the means of charitable support have been used only at the level of national agencies, universities and seminaries. Many, proven acceptable and desirable, have not been used at the level of the local church simply because there has not been either the instrumentality or the expertise to make possible their use for local mission.

We are now established to assist individuals in estate planning and the utilization of the various opportunities for philanthropic giving in our society today; and to assist in developing more adequate resources to fund work now and in the future.

You, too, can now share in this exercise of Christian stewardship which demonstrates a particular concern for mission and support for those programs at the heart of your spiritual commitment.

GIFTS

Gifts may be given in several forms: cash, securities, personal property, works of art, real estate, royalties, real property, leases from royalties, remainder life interest and appreciated property. [Such gifts may not be subject to tax as capital gains.]

Under present IRS rules you are entitled to take an immediate deduction for the full value of your gift up to 50% of your adjusted gross income for gifts of cash, and 30% for gifts of appreciated property. Sums in excess qualify as charitable contributions over as many as five succeeding years.

GIFTS OF DEFERRED VALUE

Gifts of deferred value—designated for your local church or a particular program—may provide you with significant income for as long as you live. Income is determined by the plan you choose, your age and sex. Here are several from which you may choose:

A Gift Annuity

A gift annuity irrevocable agreement with your local church would provide for you a fixed income throughout your life as well as the lifetime of a second person you may designate. The amount of income is determined by the annuity rate adopted by the National Committee on Gift Annuity tables, and varies according to age and sex.

Example: Mrs. Mary Smith, age 80, gives to her church $10,000 for a gift annuity. She is immediately entitled to a $3,956 charitable deduction. She will also receive $900 annually, of which 71.4% is tax free.

The advantages to you in this form of gift are that you will have an immediate charitable deduction for the gift value provided through the contract, and that a portion of the income you receive from the annuity will be tax exempt.

A Deferred Payment Annuity

A Deferred Payment Gift Annuity irrevocable agreement with your church or a particular program provides an immediate charitable deduction and a fixed income beginning at a *specified future date.*

Example: John Fox, age 45, gives to his church $20,000 but wishes to have the annual income begin when he is 65. There is an immediate charitable deduction on the $20,000, and when annual income is received, a percentage of each payment is tax free.

An Annuity Trust—
The Charitable Remainder

In an Annuity Trust you irrevocably transfer part of your estate to a trustee of your choice who manages the investment and pays you or a designated beneficiary a fixed income for life. Upon death the remaining principal goes to your church or the program of your choice. You determine the amount you wish to receive at the time of establishing the Trust. It must be at least 5% of the gift's initial value, but may be more. The higher the annual income, the less will be the charitable deduction.

Example: Marion Tower, age 60, transfers $100,000 to fund her Annuity Trust, and elects to receive $5,000 a year for life. Her charitable deduction is $47,312. If she wishes to receive $6,000 a year the deduction would be $35,371. The fact that no capital gains need to be paid at the time of transfer may be a special advantage.

The advantages are an immediate charitable deduction, no capital gains tax when transferring appreciated assets to the trust and an exclusion on annual income based on sex/sexes and age/ages.

A Unitrust—
The Charitable Remainder

A Unitrust, like an Annuity Trust, is created by the irrevocable transfer of cash or securities to a trustee of your choice who manages the assets **and pays the donor, or other designated beneficiary, an income for life.** In a Unitrust, however, you receive a fixed *percentage* (but not less than 5%) of the principal based on annual revaluation whereas in the Annuity Trust you receive a fixed dollar amount. In a Unitrust, capital may be added to the trust from time to time without establishing another trust agreement.

Example: Gladys Worth creates a Unitrust with $100,000 and determines that she wishes a 5% return. The first year she receives $5,000. In the second year, due to the fact that her assets have increased to $110,000 she receives $5,500. Income varies with the value of the assets.

Advantages are: a hedge against inflation, since the percentage of return is applied to the assets as they are revalued each year; an immediate charitable deduction; no capital gains tax when transferring appreciated assets to the Trust; and no unvasion of principal.

LIFE INSURANCE POLICIES

Numerous gift opportunities are available through life insurance policies. You may name The First Baptist Church of Greater Cleveland the irrevocable owner of a new or existing policy.

The gift value, for tax purposes, equals your investment in a new policy, and the cost that would be required to replace an existing policy. Premium payments qualify as charitable contributions.

You may include The First Baptist Church of Greater Cleveland as the beneficiary of a policy. At your death, the amount that is received becomes a charitable contribution in your estate.

You may assign annual dividends from your policy as a systematic way of giving tax free income on a regular basis.

YOUR WILL—
A PERMANENT MEMORIAL

The inclusion of The First Baptist Church of Greater Cleveland provides a gift from your estate and a permanent witness of your Christian concerns.

Forms that you may provide your attorney in preparing your will are:

GENERAL BEQUEST—I give and bequeath to The First Baptist Church of Greater Cleveland the sum of (amount) for the general purposes of its work.

DESIGNATED BEQUEST—I give and bequeath to The First Baptist Church of Greater Cleveland the sum of (amount) to be used for (specific purpose or program).

The Financial Development Committee of The First Baptist Church of Greater Cleveland is available to assist members and friends of the church in the use of the instrumentalities of giving described in this brochure.

For more than 150 years, The First Baptist Church of Greater Cleveland has provided a quality program of worship, study, fellowship and service for the Greater Cleveland community. It is, in fact, a very center of mission and ministry, as well over one thousand persons each week use the facilities of the church for opportunities of personal growth and development.

Now we are pleased to offer you the means to assure that First Baptist Church will continue to have a vital role in the shaping of human life in this community for many years to come.

Your personal impact of faith and witness can be extended for the cause of Christ through a careful and purposeful designing of your own exercise of Christian Stewardship.

For further information write or call:

The Business Manager
The First Baptist Church
of Greater Cleveland
3630 Fairmount Boulevard
Cleveland, Ohio 44118
(216) 932-7480

1978 National Consultation on Financial Development
31 Langefield Road
Hillsdale, New Jersey 07642 (201) 664-8890

There are two fringe benefits in the program:
- *First,* the mere announcement of the Gift Annuity Program may stimulate current support. A development officer spoke to a woman approaching her ninetieth birthday about a Gift Annuity. She listened carefully to the presentation and suggested that the executive return for a decision in several days, which he did. On the return visit the woman expressed deep appreciation for the presentation and a real concern for the organization he represented. Her decision was: "I don't believe it is right for me to take interest from your organization. How will it be if I simply write you a check for three thousand dollars?" Naturally he accepted the gift, a gift that might well never have been offered had it not been for his presentation of the Gift Annuity Plan.
- *Second,* the plan is an excellent tool for opening the door to discussing estate planning, wills, and bequests. Many pastors find it difficult to talk about a Wills Emphasis Program. Invariably some of them say: "I simply cannot approach people about their wills. I don't know where to begin. I don't know what to say." The Gift Annuity Program offers a way to open the door for a frank and illuminating discussion of the entire subject of investments, retirement income, and the final distribution of personal assets.

9

The Charitable Remainder Trust

NO DISCUSSION of financial development would be complete without providing some consideration of the Charitable Remainder Unitrust and the Charitable Remainder Annuity Trust. Both of these trusts offer attractive funding opportunities in the deferred-giving program for the charitable and religious organization, appealing to those in all walks of life who are interested in tax economies, increased income, and the ultimate benefit that their investment will bring to their church or favorite charity.

Such trusts have long been an important part of investment opportunity portfolios of colleges and universities and have been used to some extent by a number of the denominations and their agencies in the larger mission. They have been basically foreign however, to financial development in the local church. Probably not one church in a thousand has had experience with trusts, and the few exceptions are among the relatively few large, multiple-staff congregations with knowledgeable people in administration giving counsel on the various facets of deferred giving. Either kind of Charitable Remainder Trust, however, can be established for the benefit of any single church and will require little more by way of investment procedure than a trust agreement written by qualified legal counsel.

Here are several kinds of situations in which the Charitable Remainder Trust can serve individuals and particular churches.

• *Situation One.* A highly successful businessman is in his mid-forties. His annual income has increased to six figures, placing him in a high tax bracket. Over the past dozen years he has invested in an impressive portfolio of securities. Because of the capital-gains factor he is hesitant to make revisions in the portfolio and as a result his potential capital growth will become increasingly limited in the future in a reinvestment program. He is vitally interested in his church. This interest, added to the burden of his investment concern, provides a most desirable answer for both him and his church. He establishes an irrevocable charitable trust that pays him a modest income until he reaches the age of sixty-five years, after which it provides a higher income during his retirement years. It also provides him with income-tax exclusion benefits for the rest of his life. His estate tax picture, too, is greatly improved and the residual of the investment becomes the asset of his church at his demise.

• *Situation Two.* An attorney suggests to a widow that she proceed with estate planning. He recommends that she take $25,000 of appreciated securities and establish a trust. Here, also, an officer of her church serves as trustee since the residual in the trust will go to the church at the time of her death. Her first approach to designing a trust agreement was to contact the trust department of her local bank. Here she was discouraged because the institution would not handle a trust agreement in which assets were under $100,000. The trustee in the local church, representing the board of trustees of that church, through the counsel of a qualified investment broker, placed the assets in an open-end investment company that could handle investment portfolios as small as $5,000. This trust agreement provides her with an immediate tax deduction, an exclusion on a sizable portion of the annual income, a sizable tax benefit for her estate at the time of her death, and the capital remaining becomes an asset of her church when her life here comes to an end.

• *Situation Three.* A couple in their early retirement years discover that they are property poor. Most of their resources are in real estate, and their liquid assets are extremely limited. They put some of their real estate, representing $100,000, in trust. The trust sells the real estate without being required to pay taxes on the appreciated value, invests the proceeds from the sale in securities providing a reasonable return, and pays $8,000 a year to the donors for as long as they both, or either, shall live. The couple reduce their tax burden in real estate, have a benefit in gift that will qualify for the 50 percent of their income in charitable contributions with carry-over for several years, take an exclusion on a portion of their annual income for as long as either lives, and will have a distinct advantage in tax shelter on their estate when either or both die. The residual of the trust will be a distinct asset for their church and provide a meaningful memorial for family members and friends for many years to come.

• *Situation Four.* In this situation, a gentleman has been most successful in his business enterprises and is due for retirement in three years. He is concerned to maximize his retirement income without incurring capital gains taxes on his appreciated securities. Also, he wants to provide adequately for his wife should he die. He, too, consults with his attorney and the trustees of his local church. A special trust is established, providing a comfortable income for him and his wife. His Federal estate-tax liability is greatly reduced and he and his wife annually have income-tax deductions as a result of the trust. When they both expire, the residual will go to their local church.

• *Situation Five.* This gentleman was fortunate in buying a block of securities early in his business career that gained in value to almost unbelievable proportions. Because the securities are of the growth type the annual income is very small. He would like to sell them and place the money received in high-yield securities; however, the capital-gains taxes would be crushing. He and his attorney consult the trustees of his local church. He establishes a trust agreement whereby the securities are irrevocably given to the local church to be invested for his benefit. The trust is written to provide him with an annual income of $10,000 a year. The low-yield income securities are sold by the trustee, who may be a trustee of the local church as well, and there is no capital gain. His annual income has a sizable tax exclusion. At his demise the assets from the trust belong to the local church.

What are the mechanics of such a program in a local church? Because custodial fees for trust agreements by commercial organizations are great, and minimum standards high in terms of size—

usually not less than $100,000—the local church can provide for trusteeship with little or no cost to the donor. Whatever expenses are incurred are debited against the trust as current operating expenses. The local church, through proper resolutions, can make known its availability for this type of service to its membership.

The donor will be required to set up the trust agreement in terms of his capabilities and interests. He or she will instruct the attorney to prepare the trust agreement with the ultimate benefits irrevocably designated for his local church. When the trust is established, the trustee (or trustees, as the case may be) has full control of the investment portfolio. Numerous investment brokers are available to serve them, and the trust funds can be invested in open-end investment portfolios both to meet the needs of the individual and gradually to provide lasting benefits for the church. There are two types of agreements that may be written:

• The first is the Charitable Remainder Annuity Trust. In such a trust the trustees are required to provide annually to the donor (or beneficiary) a specific amount as designated in the trust. If the earnings from investments are not great enough to meet the required amount, capital will be expended to make up the difference.

As an example of this type of agreement, the donor is to receive $5,000 a year. The income from securities in trust provides $4,000 the first year, $5,200 the second year, and $4,900 the third year. In the first year the capital will be reduced by $1,000. Two hundred dollars will be added to capital the second year. One hundred dollars will be taken from the portfolio in the third year. This continues for as long as the person (or persons) lives who is to receive benefits from the trust or until a date of termination has arrived. Whatever capital remains is the property of the church or organization for which the trust was actually established.

Income to the donor in the Charitable Remainder Annuity Trust thus is fixed. An 8 percent return will provide 8 percent of the face value of the trust agreement for as long as the donor (or donors) shall live. If invested funds increase in worth 100 percent, the income to the donor or donors will not change. The converse is true as well. If the invested funds decrease in worth to 50 percent of the original investment, income to the donor or donors will remain at 8 percent annually of the sum originally placed in trust.

For the sake of clarity, it may be well to emphasize the differences between the Gift Annuity Program discussed in the preceding chapter and the Charitable Remainder Annuity Trust under discussion here. There are four basic differences:

- *First,* the Gift Annuity is an instrument defined and designed by an institution or organization in accordance with national policies accepted by religious and charitable nonprofit organizations. The Charitable Remainder Annuity Trust is defined and designed by the donor or person establishing the trust.
- *Second,* the Gift Annuity is structured to provide ultimate benefit to the institution or organization issuing the contract. In a Charitable Remainder Annuity Trust the donor, or person establishing the trust, may provide benefit to one or several charitable nonprofit institutions or organizations. In fact, the person establishing the trust may reserve the privilege of changing the trust agreement from time to time to provide residual benefit to institutions or organizations other than those named in the original trust agreement. However, institutions or organizations considered in revisions must qualify as nonprofit charitable organizations as in the first instance.
- *Third,* the income from the Gift Annuity received by the annuitant annually is determined by the rate established by the National Committee on Gift Annuities at the time the annuity is written. This is based on age and sex of the annuitant or annuitants. Gift value at the time the annuity is written and tax exclusion on the annual income are determined by those indices. In the Charitable Remainder Annuity Trust, however, the income is determined by the annuitant, or donor. The gift value and tax exclusion on annual income are determined by the age and sex of the annuitant or annuitants and the rate of return is determined by the trust. The annual return must exceed 5 percent of the amount initially provided to establish the trust.
- *Fourth,* the invested funds for the Gift Annuity are controlled and managed by the institution or organization issuing the certificate as governed by state statutes. The funds invested in a Charitable Remainder Annuity Trust are managed by the trustee named in the trust agreement. Investment policy, for income or growth, may be defined by the donor in establishing the trust.

THE CHARITABLE REMAINDER UNITRUST

IMPORTANT

This form is intended to be used exclusively by attorneys as a guide in the preparation of irrevocable charitable remainder unitrust under Section 664 of the Internal Revenue Code, which also complies with the laws of the Commonwealth of Massachusetts. The provisions setting forth beneficial interests and administrative provisions should not be completed or altered in any way except by an attorney thoroughly familiar with the requirements in this area since apparently minor changes in language may result in a loss of all tax advantages to be derived from establishing such a trust. This form was prepared with reference to laws in effect in January, 1973.

I, _____, of _____,
in the County of _____ and Commonwealth of Massachusetts, hereby deliver to
_____ of _____,
as my Trustee hereunder, the personal property listed in my Trustee's receipt of even date herewith,
which property and all additional contributions, together with any undistributed income therefrom, is hereinafter
called "the trust property," and my Trustee shall hold and administer the trust property, in trust nevertheless,
on the following terms and for the following purposes:

Article I

Definitions

As used in this instrument the words "my Trustee" shall mean the trustee for the time being in office; the words "the Code" shall mean the United States Internal Revenue Code of 1954 as the same has been, and may in the future be, amended from time to time; and the words "this instrument" and "hereunder" shall refer to this Deed of Trust.

Article II

Irrevocability

This Deed of Trust may not be revoked, modified or amended in any manner whatsoever, except as expressly provided in *Article IV.*

Article III

Disposition of Trust Property

My Trustee shall hold and dispose of the trust property as follows:

A. My Trustee shall pay to me or apply for my benefit during my lifetime, in each taxable year beginning with the date of execution of this instrument, an amount (hereinafter called the "unitrust amount") equal to *_____% of the net fair market value of the trust property, such net fair market value to be determined by my Trustee as of the date of execution of this instrument and, thereafter, on the first day of each succeeding taxable year of the trust, or as may otherwise be required by the Code or by any regulations thereunder in order to qualify the trust created hereunder as a charitable remainder unitrust as the same is defined in Section 664(d)(2) of the Code. The unitrust amount may be paid from income and/or principal as my Trustee determines, any income for a taxable year in excess of the unitrust amount to be added to principal.

B. Upon my death, my Trustee shall pay the entire balance of the trust property outright to_____
_____.

_____
*Must be at least 5%.

— 1 —

The specimen form shown on this and the following three pages was prepared for use in Massachusetts. The laws of other states may vary slightly from the procedure outlined here.

amount may be paid from income and/or principal as my Trustee determines, any income for a taxable year in excess of the annuity amount to be added to principal.

B. Upon my death, my Trustee shall pay the entire balance of the trust property outright to _____ _____.

Article IV

Administration of the Trust Created Hereunder
as a Charitable Remainder Annuity Trust

The trust created hereunder is intended to qualify as a charitable remainder annuity trust as defined in Section 664(d)(1) of the Code and is to be administered in such manner as to qualify it for exemption from taxation as is provided for a charitable remainder annuity trust under said section. To this end, without limiting the generality of the foregoing and notwithstanding any other provisions contained in this instrument to the contrary:

A. Except with regard to the annuity amount payable to me, my Trustee is prohibited from engaging in any act of self-dealing (as defined in Section 4941(d) of the Code); from making any taxable expenditures (as defined in Section 4945(d) of the Code); from retaining any excess business holdings (as defined in Section 4943(c) of the Code) which would subject this trust to tax under said Section 4943; from making any investments which would subject this trust to tax under Section 4944 of the Code; and, to the extent required, my Trustee shall pay income and principal at such times and in such manner as may be necessary to avoid subjecting this trust to tax under Section 4942 of the Code. The purpose of this paragraph A is to comply with the provisions of Section 508(e) of the Code to the extent the same are applicable to the trust hereby created.

B. If any payment to me is based upon a net fair market value of the trust property which was incorrectly determined, within a reasonable period after the final correct determination of such value my Trustee shall pay to me (in the case of an undervaluation) or shall be repaid by me (in the case of an overvaluation) an amount equal to the difference between the amount which my Trustee should have paid if the correct value had been used and the amount which my Trustee actually paid.

C. The annuity amount shall be paid to me during every taxable year prior to the date of my death, provided, however, that my Trustee shall prorate, on a daily basis, the annuity amount payable during any short taxable year and during the taxable year in which I die.

D. If, at my death, the organization named in *Article III-B* hereof is not of a type qualifying for exemption under Sections 170(c), 2055(a), and 2522 of the Code, and under the inheritance tax laws of the Commonwealth of Massachusetts, my Trustee shall distribute the trust property to such one or more organizations as are then of a type so qualifying as my Trustee shall select.

E. My Trustee may from time to time amend the provisions of this Deed of Trust for the sole purpose of enabling it to comply with Regulations which may be issued from time to time under Section 664 of the Code, and any such amendments shall apply retroactively to the creation of this Trust.

Article V

Trustee's Powers

In extension and not in limitation of the powers given by law or other provisions of this instrument, and subject to the restrictions contained in *Articles III* and *IV* and in the regulations under Section 664 of the Code, my Trustee shall have the following powers exercisable from time to time in my Trustee's discretion and may without order or license of court:

1. Retain any investments or cash, however the same may be acquired for such period of time as my Trustee shall deem advisable, and invest and reinvest in any kind of real or personal property whatsoever (including mutual funds and any common trust fund of which my Trustee hereunder is a trustee) without giving notice to any beneficiary, notwithstanding the fact that any or all thereof is of a character or size which, but for this express authority, would not be considered a proper investment for my Trustee to make;

2. Sell real or personal property at public or private sale, and exchange, lease, give options and make contracts concerning any such property for such consideration and upon such terms as to credit or otherwise as my Trustee may determine, which leases, options and contracts may extend beyond the term of the trust;

3. Give general or special proxies or powers of attorney for voting or acting in respect of securities, which may be discretionary and with power of substitution, deposit securities with, or transfer them to, protective committees or similar bodies, join in any reorganization and pay assessments or subscriptions called for in connection with securities held by my Trustee;

4. Hold securities in bearer form, in the name of my Trustee, in street name or in the name of a nominee or nominees, hold real estate in the name of a nominee or nominees and maintain bank accounts without indication of any fiduciary capacity;

5. Keep any or all of the property of the trust at any place or places within or without the Commonwealth of Massachusetts or with a depositary or custodian at such place or places;

6. Employ as investment counsel, custodians, brokers, accountants, appraisers, attorneys or other agents such persons, firms or organizations, including my Trustee and any firm or organization of which my Trustee may be a member or employee, as my Trustee may deem necessary or desirable any pay as an expense of the administration of the trust the reasonable compensation of such persons, firms or organizations;

7. Take or defend any proceedings at law or in equity with reference to or in any matter concerning the trust, represent the interests of the trust in any proceedings with power to settle, compromise and refer to arbitration any matter in any way affecting the same and pay, compromise or contest any other claim or dispute directly or indirectly affecting the property of the trust; and

8. Sign, seal, acknowledge and deliver all instruments and take any steps and do any acts which my Trustee may deem necessary or proper in connection with the due care, management and disposition of the trust property.

Article VII

Trustee's Accounts

My Trustee shall render annually an accounting of the administration of the trust created hereunder to me and to the organization named in *Article III-B* hereof, and our written approval shall, as to all transactions shown in such accounting, be final and binding on all persons and organizations (whether the identity thereof is known or not) who are then or may thereafter become entitled to receive any distribution hereunder. The failure to object to such accounting within sixty days after the receipt thereof shall be deemed to be the equivalent of written approval of the person or organization receiving the same.

Article VIII

Resignation and Appointment of Trustees

Any trustee hereunder may resign by an instrument in writing delivered or mailed to me during my lifetime. In the event of a vacancy for any reason in the office of trustee hereunder, a successor trustee shall be appointed by me if I am then living, or, if I am not then living, by the organization named in *Article III-B* hereof. In each case such appointment shall be by an instrument in writing and shall become effective upon the written acceptance of the appointee.

Article IX

Restriction on Alienation

Neither the income nor the principal of this trust shall be alienable by any beneficiary, either by anticipation, assignment, or by any other method, and the same shall not be subject to be taken by any beneficiary's creditors by any process whatever.

—3—

Article X

Governing Law

This trust is created under and shall in all respect be governed by the laws of the Commonwealth of Massachusetts.

IN WITNESS WHEREOF, I, the said _____ , have hereunto set my hand and seal this ____ day of _____ , 197__.

_____

- -

COMMONWEALTH OF MASSACHUSETTS

County of _____ , 197____

Then personally appeared the above-named _____ and acknowledged the foregoing instrument to be _____ free act and deed,

Before me,

_____

Notary Public

My commission expires:

In token of _____ acceptance of the trust hereinabove set forth, the said _____ has hereto set _____ hand and seal on this _____ day of _____ , 197___.

_____

Trustee

— 4 —

- The second type of agreement is the Charitable Remainder Unitrust. In the Unitrust a percentage of annual return based on the market value of the securities each year is written into the trust agreement. This percentage is determined by the donor and can be for any amount, providing that it is not less than 5 percent. Seldom are trust agreements written for more than 10 percent. Assume, for example, that the amount placed in trust is $100,000 and the return defined in the agreement is 6 percent. The first year the trust is worth $100,000 and the trust pays to the donor $6,000. The second year the trust is valued at $110,000. The trust in that year will provide to the donor an income of $6,600. The third year the value reduces to $105,000. The income to the donor the third year will be $6,300. Should income to the trust fall below a 6 percent return on its face value in any year, the difference will be made up from capital. In any event the amount remaining at the expiration of the trust or the demise of the donor is the property of the church.

The regulations under which Charitable Remainder Annuity Trust and Unitrust agreements are set up require that the ultimate beneficiary be a religious or charitable organization, although the agreement may be written in such a way that the donor can re-designate the proceeds from one organization to another. While such trusts have their purpose, it seems probable that a local church should not be a party to an agreement that provides the option of redesignation to the donor, if one of its trustees is going to serve as the registered trustee for the trust. The agreement must be irrevocable in order to be a charitable trust; and it is reasonable that it be irrevocable in terms of the particular organization in order that there be no disappointments, especially of a local church, along the way.

While the Charitable Remainder trust agreements are well worth considering as a part of the total support resources available to the local church, it is true that the overseeing of such an agreement does require more financial expertise at the local level than does the Gift Annuity Plan. Except in the most unusual circumstances, the responsibility for handling the trust should be contracted to a qualified institution or agency. When developing such a program a local church should contract and make public the investment procedures that will be followed in administering trust

THE CHARITABLE REMAINDER ANNUITY TRUST

IMPORTANT

This form is intended to be used exclusively by attorneys as a guide in the preparation of an irrevocable charitable remainder annuity trust under Section 664 of the Internal Revenue Code, which also complies with the laws of the Commonwealth of Massachusetts. The provisions setting forth beneficial interests and administrative provisions should not be completed or altered in any way except by an attorney thoroughly familiar with the requirements listed in this area since apparently minor changes in language may result in a loss of all tax advantages to be derived from establishing such a trust. This form was prepared with reference to laws in effect in January, 1973.

I, _____, of _____,

in the County of _____ and Commonwealth of Massachusetts, hereby deliver to

_____ of _____,

as my Trustee hereunder, the personal property listed in my Trustee's receipt of even date herewith, which property, together with any undistributed income therefrom, is hereinafter called "the trust property," and my Trustee shall hold and administer the trust property, in trust nevertheless, on the following terms and for the following purposes:

Article I

Definitions

As used in this instrument the words "my Trustee" shall mean the trustee for the time being in office; the words "the Code" shall mean the United States Internal Revenue Code of 1954 as the same has been, and may in the future be, amended from time to time; and the words "this instrument" and "hereunder" shall refer to this Deed of Trust.

Article II

Irrevocability

This Deed of Trust may not be revoked, modified or amended in any manner whatsoever except as expressly provided in Article IV E, and no property may be added to the trust hereby created after the execution hereof.

Article III

Disposition of Trust Property

My Trustee shall hold and dispose of the trust property as follows:

A. My Trustee shall pay to me or apply for my benefit during my lifetime, in each taxable year beginning with the date of execution of this instrument, an amount (hereinafter called the "annuity amount") equal to the greater of $_____ or _____%* of the initial net fair market value of the trust property, such initial net fair market value to be determined by my Trustee as of the date of execution of this instrument. The annuity

*Percentage must be at least 5%.

— 1 —

The specimen form shown on this and the following three pages was prepared for use in Massachusetts. The laws of other states may vary slightly from the procedure outlined here.

Article IV

**Administration of the Trust Created Hereunder
as a Charitable Remainder Unitrust**

The trust created hereunder is intended to qualify as a charitable remainder unitrust as defined in Section 664(d)(2) of the Code and is to be administered in such manner as to qualify it for exemption from taxation as is provided for a charitable remainder unitrust under said section. To this end, without limiting the generality of the foregoing and notwithstanding any other provisions contained in this instrument to the contrary:

A. Except with regard to the unitrust amount payable to me, my Trustee is prohibited from engaging in any act of self-dealing (as defined in Section 4941(d) of the Code); from making any taxable expenditures (as defined in Section 4945(d) of the Code); from retaining any excess business holdings (as defined in Section 4943(c) of the Code) which would subject this trust to tax under said Section 4943; from making any investments which would subject this trust to tax under Section 4944 of the Code; and, to the extent required, my Trustee shall pay income and principal at such times and in such manner as may be necessary to avoid subjecting this trust to tax under Section 4942 of the Code. The purpose of this paragraph A is to comply with the provisions of Section 508(e) of the Code to the extent the same are applicable to the trust hereby created.

B. If any payment to me is based upon a net fair market value of the trust property which was incorrectly determined, within a reasonable period after the final correct determination of such value my Trustee shall pay to me (in the case of an undervaluation) or shall be repaid by me (in the case of an overvaluation) an amount equal to the difference between the amount which my Trustee should have paid if the correct value had been used and the amount which my Trustee actually paid.

C. The unitrust amount shall be paid to me during every taxable year prior to the date of my death, *provided, however,* that my Trustee shall prorate, on a daily basis, the unitrust amount payable during any short taxable year and during the taxable year in which I die.

D. If, at my death, the organization named in *Article III-B* hereof is not of a type qualifying for exemption under Sections 170(c), 2055(a), and 2522 of the Code, and under the inheritance tax laws of the Commonwealth of Massachusetts, my Trustee shall distribute the trust property to such one or more organizations as are then of a type so qualifying as my Trustee shall select.

E. For purposes of the taxable year of the Trust in which an additional contribution is made:

1. If there is no valuation date after the time of such contribution and during the taxable year in which such contribution is made, the additional property shall be valued at the time of contribution, and

2. The unitrust amount for such taxable year shall be computed by multiplying ____ %* by the sum of (a) the net fair market value of the Trust's assets (excluding the value of the additional property and any income from and any appreciation on such property after its contribution) and (b) that proportion of the value of the additional property (that was excluded under subdivision (a) of this subparagraph) which the number of days in the period which begins with the date of contribution and ends with the earlier of (1.) the last day of the taxable year during which such contribution is made, and (2.) the date of my death, bears to the number of days in the period which begins with the first day of such taxable year and ends with the earlier of (1.) the last day in such taxable year, and (2.) the date of my death.

F. My Trustee may from time to time amend the provisions of this Deed of Trust for the sole purpose of enabling it to comply with Regulations which may be issued from time to time under Section 664 of the Code, and any such amendments shall apply retroactively to the creation of this Trust.

Article V

Trustee's Powers

In extension and not in limitation of the powers given by law or other provisions of this instrument, and subject to the restrictions contained in *Articles III* and *IV* and in the regulations under Section 664 of the Code, my Trustee shall have the following powers exercisable from time to time in my Trustee's discretion and may without order or license of court: _____

---

*Same percentage as on page 1.

1. Retain any investments or cash, however the same may be acquired for such period of time as my Trustee shall deem advisable, and invest and reinvest in any kind of real or personal property whatsoever (including mutual funds and any common trust fund of which my Trustee hereunder is a trustee) without giving notice to any beneficiary, notwithstanding the fact that any or all thereof is of a character or size which, but for this express authority, would not be considered a proper investment for my Trustee to make;

2. Sell real or personal property at public or private sale, and exchange, lease, give options and make contracts concerning any such property for such consideration and upon such terms as to credit or otherwise as my Trustee may determine, which leases, options and contracts may extend beyond the term of the Trust;

3. Give general or special proxies or powers of attorney for voting or acting in respect of securities, which may be discretionary and with power of substitution, deposit securities with, or transfer them to, protective committees or similar bodies, join in any reorganization and pay assessments or subscriptions called for in connection with securities held by my Trustee;

4. Hold securities in bearer form, in the name of my Trustee, in street name or in the name of a nominee or nominees, hold real estate in the name of a nominee or nominees and maintain bank accounts without indication of any fiduciary capacity;

5. Keep any or all of the property of the trust at any place or places within or without the Commonwealth of Massachusetts or with a depositary or custodian at such place or places;

6. Employ as investment counsel, custodians, brokers, accountants, appraisers, attorneys or other agents such persons, firms or organizations, including my Trustee and any firm or organization of which my Trustee may be a member or employee, as my Trustee may deem necessary or desirable any pay as an expense of the administration of the trust the reasonable compensation of such persons, firms or organizations;

7. Take or defend any proceedings at law or in equity with reference to or in any matter concerning the trust, represent the interests of the trust in any proceedings with power to settle, compromise and refer to arbitration any matter in any way affecting the same and pay, compromise or contest any other claim or dispute directly or indirectly affecting the property of the trust; and

8. Sign, seal, acknowledge and deliver all instruments and take any steps and do any acts which my Trustee may deem necessary or proper in connection with the due care, management and disposition of the trust property.

Article VII

Trustee's Accounts

My Trustee shall render annually an accounting of the administration of the trust created hereunder to me and to the organization named in *Article III-B* hereof, and our written approval shall, as to all transactions shown in such accounting, be final and binding on all persons and organizations (whether the identity thereof is known or not) who are then or may thereafter become entitled to receive any distribution hereunder. The failure to object to such accounting within sixty days after the receipt thereof shall be deemed to be the equivalent of the written approval of the person or organization receiving the same.

Article VIII

Resignation and Appointment of Trustees

Any trustee hereunder may resign by an instrument in writing delivered or mailed to me during my life-time. In the event of a vacancy for any reason in the office of trustee hereunder, a successor trustee shall be appointed by me if I am then living, or, if I am not then living, by the organization named in *Article III-B* hereof. In each case such appointment shall be by an instrument in writing and shall become effective upon the written acceptance of the appointee.

Article IX

Restriction on Alienation

Neither the income nor the principal of this trust shall be alienable by any beneficiary, either by antᵢ. pation, assignment, or by any other method, and the same shall not be subject to be taken by any beneficiary's creditors by any process whatever.

Article X

Governing Law

This trust is created under and shall in all respects be governed by the laws of the Commonwealth of Massachusetts.

IN WITNESS WHEREOF, I, the said _____ ,
have hereunto set my hand and seal this ___ day of _____, 197

- -

COMMONWEALTH OF MASSACHUSETTS

County of _____ , 197____

Then personally appeared the above-named _____
and acknowledged the foregoing instrument to be _____ free act and deed,
Before me,

_____
Notary Public

My commission expires:

In token of _____ acceptance of the trust hereinabove set forth, the said _____
has hereto set _____ hand and seal on this _____ day of_____, 197___.

_____
Trustee

TRUSTEE'S RECEIPT

The undersigned, as Trustee of The _____ Charitable Remainder Annuity Trust, hereby acknowledges receipt of the property listed below to be held and disposed of in accordance with the terms and provisions of the aforesaid Deed of Trust.

Date:_____, 197___.

_____

agreements for which the local church, its board of trustees, or an office is named trustee. Only in this way can a church provide the confidence in its procedures that is essential if a trust program is to be successful.

10

Life Insurance and Property

LIFE IS CHANGE and the circumstances of life change through the years. Thirty-four years ago a newly married man assumed responsibility for the support of his wife for as many years as she might live. Hopefully he would sustain health, strength, and life through that period. Incidents of diseases, accident or handicap could occur, however. While his capability might flag, responsibility for her would persist. With each child his responsibility would increase, and there would seem no alternative but to increase his insurance coverage to provide the support that would be required in the event that he himself was not able to provide. As the family increased in size, insurance was increased as well.

Now his family is raised, all are married, and each has attained a measure of professional proficiency. While a large estate may seem desirable, it is not necessarily contingent to insurance policies, and future security is not dependent upon them, either. As through a number of years it was important to increase insurance protection, the time of life has now come in which it may be wise to reduce insurance coverage. The cancellation of policies is not always the desirable course, however. The acceptance of paid-up insurance is often a reasonable alternative. Support of the local church, through insurance, may prove to be the best answer. If not always the best answer, it will at least be among the best.

There are several courses a person might take in using his insurance policies to benefit his local church.

• *First*, he may irrevocably make the local church the beneficiary of the policy. In this event the replacement value becomes deductible for income-tax purposes, and the payment of future premiums is deductible as well. Should the gift value of the policy exceed the amount one may declare as a contribution in preparing his annual tax return in that particular year, he can carry the gift value over as many as five succeeding years.

• *Second*, he may make the insurance policy a gift to his local church. If, in connection with the gift, the trustees decide to continue the policy in force by assuming the payment of the premiums from the church treasury, they can do so. Here, too, the policy beneficiary would become the local church and the assignment would be irrevocable. At the time of death the face value of the policy, together with whatever earned dividends may be available, would become the asset of the local church. For tax purposes there are two choices for the donor: he has the option of selecting either the cash value of the policy or the replacement value of the policy, whichever would provide the greater benefit.

• *Third*, let us suppose that the donor is in possession of a single policy, perhaps as large as a hundred thousand dollars. He does not choose to place the entire asset in the hands of the trustees of the local church since he continues to have a need for some insurance coverage. He may never be in a position to relinquish all such protection. He has two alternatives: First, he can turn the policy over to the church with the agreement that a portion of it be contracted to be paid to his estate at the time of his death. The portion retained for estate benefit, of course, would not be eligible either for a gift-value deduction or tax exclusion, as the case may be. The portion becoming the irrevocable gift to the church, however, would qualify for tax benefits as defined by the Internal Revenue Code. Second, if the donor questions the wisdom of making an agreement with the local church that would restrict part of the investment for the benefit of his estate, he could instead present the policy to his insurance company, requesting that it be replaced by two certificates—the size of which could be designated by him. Perhaps one would be for $75,000 and the other for $25,000. Either of them could then be presented to the local church irrevocably, and the value for income-tax purposes in gift and exclusion would be determined by whichever policy was given.

These matters should be checked out carefully by the donor with his legal counsel, because, under certain circumstances, there could be benefit, tax wise, to the estate at the time of the demise of the individual.

Gifts of insurance are not one-time gifts. Because a donor has assigned a particular policy to his local church does not mean that further assignments will not be made. There are cases in which an individual has revised his insurance portfolio as many as five times and each time benefits have accrued to the donor's local church. These revisions, of course, have not been made in a manner of months. Usually such procedures span a decade or two. However, administrators must repeatedly make options known to parishioners so that the church may be included among the donors' grants.

At his time of life—namely, the advanced years—other assets in terms of real and personal property are possible gifts for the church as well. Some donors and members, moving from their own homes to apartments, condominiums, or institutions for the aged, find it possible and advantageous to present their homes as gifts to the local church. Here, too, there are options:

- *First*, a person may contribute his home to the church outright. Here he may be eligible for several tax benefits. There are no capital gains in appreciated value. The gift value may be spread over as many as six years—that is, the year in which the gift is presented as well as the five succeeding years.
- *Second*, a person may contribute his home to the church reserving the right of occupancy for so long as the donor may live. It is important to make certain that a contract agreement of this type clearly defines the responsibility of the donor, or donors, as occupant(s) of the property, as well as the responsibility of the church receiving the gift. There are matters of taxes, upkeep, utilities, insurance, etc. All matters of risk must be borne by the donor. If it is a simple agreement in which the donor continues to assume upkeep and all expenses as previously assumed during the time of his ownership, the standard of upkeep should be specifically defined.
- *Third*, a person may contribute his home to the church in exchange for a Unitrust or Annuity Trust. Such agreements should be contingent on the sale of the property, and the trust agreement

should be written for the actual sum received as a result of the sale. Some churches have been known to enter into trust agreements based on appraised value, only to discover that they had a property on their hands that just would not sell or when sold would provide inadequate compensation for the trust agreement. Therefore, agreements should be contingent on the sale of the property and defined as providing benefits based upon the actual realized gift. It is difficult to overemphasize the importance of this. Often pastors, administrators, and trustees take the position that you cannot look a gift horse in the mouth or that the institution cannot be too particular when it comes to a donor's gift. For heaven's sake don't run the risk of possible embarrassment to a donor, his family and friends, or embarrassment to the institution, its leaders and members, by not ensuring that every gift of this type is honorable of the name and well qualified as tribute to the glory of God.

A word may also be added here concerning personal property that may be left or given to the local church. This falls into three categories:

1. Some because of their commitment to Christ and desire for benefits under the Internal Revenue Code will be pleased to make outright gifts of personal property in terms of automobiles, jewelry, furniture, and so on. There should be no strings attached, and the organization should make it a policy to convert all such personal property into cash as soon as possible.

2. There will be those who have no dependents or survivors, and they will stipulate that their personal, as well as real, property go to the local church. This, too, should be converted to cash as soon as possible.

3. Others (survivors of a parent or friend) because of distance or other involvements will not want to deal with the disposition of personal property left to them. For tax benefit they would prefer to give it to the local church, often where the parent or friend worshipped, so that the church may profit by it and relieve them of the responsibility of disposing of the same. These properties also should be converted into cash as soon as possible.

As a matter of self-discipline the local church should not itself endeavor to sell the properties or manage the distribution of personal goods. This will tend to make for an unmanageable burden in parish life and a breeding area for schism and conflict.

The disposition of personal and real property should be contracted to a broker who will be responsible for the same.

The local church needs periodically to make known to both its members and its friends that it is capable of, and prepared for, receiving gifts of real and personal property from living donors and through bequests. As these treasures become a gift to God it is the only way I know of in which a person can in a sense "take his money with him."

11

Wills and Bequests

PERHAPS NOTHING in local church programming is so neglected as stewardship in the area of deferred giving. In 1971 the North American Interchurch Study of approximately 3,500 persons discovered that only 56 percent of the clergy sample and 44 percent of the laity sample had made wills. Most studies have produced more startling reports. Many studies report as few as 3 percent have made wills. Whether 97 percent, 56 percent or 44 percent—the fact that a majority, or at least a sizable minority, of the population do not have wills is a demonstration of poor stewardship.

Significant steps need be taken. Philanthropic giving increased from $20 billion in 1970 to $43 billion in 1980. Bequests represented 11 percent of the 1970 figure and 5.4 percent of the 1980 figure. Reduction in estate taxes makes a noticeable difference.

Yet, again according to the North American Interchurch Study, 73.6 percent of the clergy and 84.6 percent of the laity have not included a bequest to their church in their will. The vast majority reported that it simply had not occurred to them at the time.

Why is the local church so remiss in this area of its local mission?

There are several reasons: *a*) most church planning is short term, *b*) immediate funding is essential, *c*) income through bequests seems remote, and *d*) emphasis on wills is near the bottom of local-church program priorities.

What incentive is there to develop a Wills-Emphasis Program when planning is short range and parish leadership is of limited tenure? There is incentive in that through a Wills-Emphasis Program a local church may not be as far from money as it assumes.

When proper programs have been developed in local churches one-half of 1 percent, based on giving units, have provided bequest income in the first year. The level increased to 1 percent the second year and to 2 percent the third year. After a number of years the bequest level may be expected to stabilize at 3.6 percent based on giving units. If the local church organization is more than fifty years old, however, the projection can be doubled; and if it is located in a community of under 5,000 inhabitants, it can be increased by another 30 percent.

Dr. Harry Emerson Fosdick had a rule that no printed material would go out from the Riverside Church without the words, "Remember Riverside Church in your will," imprinted on it. An average of a quarter of a million dollars annually is received by Riverside Church from members whose wills were written during the years of his pastoral ministry.

What constitutes a good Wills-Emphasis Program in a local church?

• *First*, a simple beginning is to adopt Dr. Fosdick's rule. Annual membership directories, newsletters, and publications can carry the line: "Remember your church in your will."

• *Second*, forms for designated, as well as undesignated, bequests should be provided in some of the publications. The annual report to the membership may be one and the directory of church members may be another. The forms given below, with suitable variations, may be used:

GENERAL BEQUEST

I give and bequeath to *(name of organization)*, incorporated *(date)* in the state of *(name of state)* the sum of *(amount)* for the general purposes of its work.

DESIGNATED BEQUEST

I give and bequeath to *(name of organization)*, incorporated *(date)* in the state of *(name of state)* the sum of *(amount)* to be used for *(purpose of program)*.

- *Third,* literature should be distributed periodically to the members to assist them in fiscal procedures and estate planning. The National Consultation on Financial Development has a "Data Bank" that is available at modest cost. It may be used to list important data, including members of family, Social Security number, insurance policy numbers, bank accounts, depositories, stocks and bonds, along with preferences concerning a memorial service and disposition of the remains. On the back of the brochure there may be a check list of methods of support for the local church. Such a listing may include:

_____ A bequest in my will.

_____ A gift of cash.

_____ A gift of securities.

_____ A gift of life insurance.

_____ A gift annuity.

_____ A Unitrust for myself, spouse, and church.

_____ Life income provided by my church's pooled income fund.

Directly below are forms for general and designated bequests.

Similar brochures of this type, which offer an opportunity for personalizing the message by providing space in which to imprint the name and address of the local church, are available from many denominational boards, ecumenical agencies, and church supply houses. Distribution should be programmed regularly.

- *Fourth,* seminars in estate planning should be scheduled from time to time in every congregation. Different age groups should be brought together at different times to discuss the special problems of estate planning of vital interest to them in their particular place in the life cycle. Groupings may include couples, couples with families, recently married, mid-life and fifty-plus as well as single young, single mid-life, and single fifty-plus. Seminars for those soon to retire as well as for those who have retired are always in order. Leadership for these events may be drawn very frequently right out of the parish. Lawyers, accountants, social workers, trust officers in banking institutions, and counselors are in a position to do a good job in these areas. Most denominations, and some ecumenical organizations, have qualified personnel and the necessary audiovisual resources and materials to interpret needs, concerns, and alerts.

- *Fifth,* the pulpit, supplemented by pastoral counseling and personal visitation, is essential. The well-rounded homiletical schedule will include sermons on stewardship as often as ten times a year, with at least one sermon being on the stewardship of resources beyond one's years. With the present emphasis on ecology, the stewardship of resources is very much at home in the topical environment. One minister rewrites his will twice each year. As a result, in pastoral visitation, it becomes a commonplace for him to mention that he revised his will recently, as one subject among other subjects such as new cars, new television sets, new clothes, and new things. The conversation flows quite easily from the pastor's will to the parishioner's need for good will-planning.

- *Sixth,* visitation teams in Wills-Emphasis Programs are in order, providing the team members have credibility. Having developed a profile for each giving unit in the parish, teams may select units appropriate for this emphasis at a seemingly proper time. Their visit should include an emphasis on the importance of doing the job right, obtaining good counsel from professionals, and assuming responsible stewardship for the future. Remembering the church in one's will should not be the primary emphasis. Instead, this should simply assume its proper place among those things for which a Christian is truly responsible.

- *Seventh,* some churches have found it possible to serve as a depository for wills. Many individuals, especially those residing alone with no close relatives near by, welcome the privilege of having their will in the church's vault or safe. These documents, of course, are confidential, and filing systems should be arranged so that a parishioner can seal his will within a uniform envelope furnished by the church. Thus the envelope will not be difficult to handle in sorting it with others in your facility. If the church does not have a safe or vault it can contract for the same at a local bank.

- *Eighth,* a church may provide sample will forms for members. These should not be distributed to encourage a "do it yourself" program; however, many people have never seen a will, have no idea what is included in a typical will, and may be encouraged to act if they have opportunity to become acquainted with the document and the process.

- *Ninth,* a church may maintain a Wills-Emphasis Roster. The roster may be in a volume, similar to a Book of Remembrance for Memorials and Gifts, or a framed wall document under glass on which are listed the names of those who have remembered the church in their will. One church awards a golden harp lapel pin to each person providing a copy of his bequest to the church to be placed in its archives. One Sunday each year is set aside to make the presentations in public. If any person has reservations about receiving the pin in public, he may receive it privately and no announcement or publicity is given the fact.

A local church never knows of all the wills in which it is included or the value of bequests that may come to it in time. As personal situations change, will revisions should be made. It is important that the local church emphasize the revising of wills as well as the writing of a first document.

Strange as it may seem, 25 percent of those leaving funds to local churches are not active participants in the church's program at the time of their demise. Some have changed their place of residence. Some have even changed their church membership. Nevertheless their will makes articulate their interest and zeal for the church they have remembered in their will.

The Wills-Emphasis Program through the years can increase annual support substantially. If properly done it cannot fail to produce resources in a comparatively short time.

12

A New Age of Plastic Currency and Computer Processing

WE MAY OR MAY NOT be favorably impressed with plastic currency and computer processing; however, they occupy a significant role in our economy and have a major function in fiscal funds transfers. Certainly organized religion cannot expect to have a reasonable share of financial support in the future without them.

Often we are critical of the support given religion by our members. Yet many believe that such limited support is related to the church's unwillingness to move into new dimensions of support such as the authorization of a check or bank funds transfer.

For too many years we have been singing:

> "Dropping, dropping, dropping, dropping,
> Hear the pennies fall;
> Every one for Jesus,
> He will get them all!"

The pennies drop in the Sunday-school offering basket, in the Women's Circle offering of the "least coin," and in the Sunday morning service where the "coin of the realm" is very much at home in limited support of the church's mission.

In Buffalo, New York, the Coronation of the Blessed Virgin Mary Church announced that it could no longer survive on fifty-cent contributions. It introduced bank-card procedures. Transactions through plastic currency now vary from fifteen to thirty dollars per family. Total parish income increased by 300 percent in the first quarter.

Following an address to churchmen largely carrying administrative responsibilities for large parishes in the Tulsa, Oklahoma, area, William Neff, Jr., introduced bank-card giving to St. Andrew's Presbyterian Church there. In a matter of weeks the metropolitan newspaper announced that bank cards had become a way of life in the support of St. Andrew's Church.

How can it be done? Must clerks sit at desks in the narthex, fill out forms, and pass the plastic bank cards through the embossing machine for processing? Certainly not. A local church commitment and the transaction itself are as simple as ordering items from the *Shopper's Guide* on an airplane. In proper forms the donor lists his name, the commitment in terms of a single transaction or a program of transactions spanning months or years, and lists the identification numbers on his account with MasterCard or VISA. *Note:* Before implementing the procedure the local church must make arrangements with the local banking institutions to ensure that they will honor documents as authorized and presented.

What does it cost? There is little cost to the local church. Enrollment is gratis. The transaction fee usually begins at 5.1% of funds transferred in a monthly period with a minimum of $3.50. The transaction fee reduces as the volume of dollars increases each month.

There are, of course, those who do not believe that a church should be involved in credit processes that may impose difficult burdens on communicants. High pressure is never in order; however, a bank card is not a credit process unless the transaction is converted to a deferred payment plan. In other words, a donor whose account is paid in full within twenty-six days of the billing has engaged in the process with no cost to himself. It is, indeed, a transfer of funds from his bank account to the account of the local church.

The Windward United Church of Christ in Kailua, Hawaii, has developed a "Mahalo" or "Thank you" Card for those who have taken this step in local church support. It is available in the narthex and is placed in the offering plate by the contributor, if he so desires, as a gesture of solidarity with all who are contributing to the support of their church.

MAHALO CARD

Thank you for supporting your Church in the modern manner. Please place this Mahalo Card in collection plate as a symbol of your thoughtful gift and your participation in the offertory.

Name _____ Date _____

The use of this card permits those who have pledged through programmed giving to participate in the offertory ritual.

Programmed giving should not exceed three years. Arrangements can be made "until forbid" but this closes the door, it seems to me, to a periodical review of the contribution level of the communicant. At least once in three years a communicant should be challenged to raise his sights and review the mission of the church.

AUTOGIVE, pre-authorized electronic funds transfers, must be introduced to the local church. AUTOGIVE may begin with a pilot group forming a giving pattern programmed monthly over a three-month period. Funds may be transferred on the fifth or twentieth day of the month as administration elects. Progress reports must be shared with the parish monthly.

When the pilot program has been initiated and a track record established over a period of two or three months, the procedure may be introduced to the total parish with testimonials provided by those involved in the pilot program.

Consider the AUTOGIVE experience in these churches where authorizations on a regular monthly basis assure financial support to the local church:

In this totally voluntary procedure the treasurer can be sure

RECORD OF GIVING THROUGH AUTOGIVE

	City/State	Average authorization per donor per year
CHURCH INSTITUTION		
Peekskill United Methodist	Peekskill, New York	$2,785.32
Christ Episcopal Church	Tarrytown, New York	801.00
Bolton Federated	Bolton, Massachusetts	1,050.00
First Presbyterian	York, Pennsylvania	700.36
Garden City United Methodist	Monroeville, Pennsylvania	1,874.04
Stone United Methodist	McKeesport, Pennsylvania	517.20
Waynedale United Methodist	Fort Wayne, Indiana	804.96
Castleton United Methodist	Indianapolis, Indiana	900.00
First Baptist	Cleveland, Ohio	862.68
Littleton United Methodist	Littleton, Colorado	988.08
New Hope Christian	Boise, Idaho	950.04
Woodland Hills Community	Woodland Hills, California	493.80
Iao Congregational	Wailuku, Maui, Hawaii	696.12
AGENCY		
Queens Federation of Churches	Richmond Hills, New York	$ 120.00
Presbyterian Senior Services	New York, New York	180.00
Bread for the World	Washington, D.C.	130.68
Council of Churches	Buffalo, New York	113.88
Project Equality	Kansas City, Missouri	600.00
Portland Youth for Christ	Portland, Oregon	190.00

when funds will be available to meet the local church's obligations. Funds are available the day the local church selects; it may be the fifth or twentieth day of each month.

AUTOGIVE IS . . .

- A banking process whereby donors may order their church commitment paid automatically by their bank.

- A thoughtful action by responsible Christians who want to assure ministry and mission through regular, systematic giving.

- Convenient for donors - - no checks to write or mail.

- Helpful in reducing administrative expense while assuring support even when you must be away, weather threatens or illness strikes.

- Easy to use. Merely complete the simple form and we'll do the rest.

- Safely regulated by banking laws. You may terminate participation at any time.

- Now used by thousands and available to you in making your church commitment even more helpful.

MAY

WE

SUGGEST . . . . .

. . . . AUTOGIVE

a thoughtful tool of
Christian Philanthropy
for the 21st Century.

AUTOGIVE information and authorization form for the local church.

AUTOGIVE CONDITIONS

This authorization to charge my account shall be the same as if I personally signed a check to the church.

A record of my payment will be included in my bank statement. This record will serve as my receipt.

I have the right to authorize my bank to reverse any erroneous entry. This must be done by written notice within 15 days of the date of the bank statement or within 45 days after the debit was made.

I may terminate my participation in this process upon written notification to the church.

All information is strictly confidential.

WOODLAND HILLS
COMMUNITY CHURCH
21338 Dumetz Road
Woodland Hills, CA 91364
346-0820

AUTHORIZATION FORM

I hereby authorize my bank to charge my account each month and pay the Church the amount shown in accordance with the conditions on the reserve side of this form.

Monthly Amount: $ _____

Date: _____

Signature: _____

Address: _____

City/State/Zip: _____

ATTACH A CHECK MARKED 'VOID' FOR THE ACCOUNT TO BE DEBITED EACH MONTH.

Your account will be debited on the 20th day of each month.

Mail this form to the Church Office. A copy will be returned to you.

The cost of the program is modest. A church with less than a thousand members (or an organization with a budget under $100,000) may enroll for fifty dollars. Larger organizations will pay $100. Each authorization has a fifty-cent start-up fee. Monthly funds transfers, with full cumulative reporting to the local church, or agency, cost a modest twenty cents per transaction. The program has been developed, and is administered by, The National Consultation on Financial Development, 31 Langerfeld Road, Hillsdale, N.J., 07642 (201/664-8890).

Over forty million people receive their salaries and retirement income from the United States Treasury through electronic funds transfer. In April 1985, 18,370,000 persons received Social Security Benefits through DIRECT DEPOSIT. At the time this represented forty percent of the 45,892,836 persons receiving Social Security Payments. Persons electing electronic funds transfers increase in number each month. This is a trend no local church can afford to ignore.

As more sophisticated funds transfer systems are introduced into the community, the local church will need to engage in more sophisticated pilot programs. For example, the Seattle–First National Bank has experimented with an amazing information system that linked a home pushbutton telephone to a high-speed computer when the computer number was dialed. Once the computer answered, the subscriber's file number was entered into the system by verbal command and these six valuable services were instantly available:

—Checkless Bill Payment
—Updating Family Budget
—Income Tax Programming
—Personal Calendar Needs
—Household Records
—Mathematical Procedures

The experiment was recessed after six months for two basic reasons: First, only 20 percent of the Seattle area telephone users had pushbutton instruments. Second, along with this rather limited market, too few merchants held membership in the pool as firms to whom bills could be paid. To work properly and economi-

In the In-Touch system, a simple template fits over the face of the subscriber's pushbutton telephone, transforming it into the keyboard of a sophisticated calculating machine.

cally, the system required the more sophisticated instrument and comprehensive training in an educational process for users. Nevertheless, such telephone computing service is the fact of the future. It is a next step beyond our present cash-paying and check-writing society.

Indeed, as early as May 1973 the Mitre Corporation introduced plans for interactive television, which combined the pushbutton telephone with cable TV. This work was supported by the National Science Foundation Grant GJ–32785. Peter F. Drucker in *The Age of Discontinuity* stated: "There is no technical reason why someone like Sears Roebuck should not come out tomorrow with an appliance selling for less than a TV set, capable of being plugged in wherever there is electricity, and giving immediate access to all the information needed."

Michael J. Dunn, Assistant Vice-President and Manager for Electronic Funds Transfer Services for United Jersey Banks, is responsible for an amazing information system they offer their

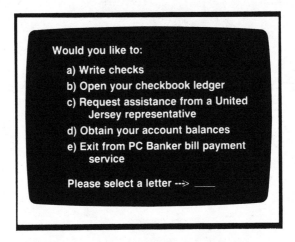

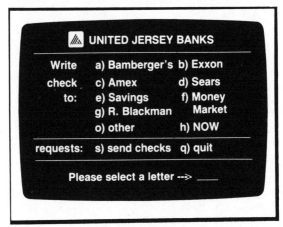

A portion of the menu prepared by United Jersey Banks for personal computer usage.

customers. The system links a customer's personal home computer to the bank's high-speed computer when the telephone number is dialed. Once the computer answers, the customer's bank account number and Personal Identification Number are automatically entered and five valuable services are instantly available:

- *Bill Payments.* Programmed into the bank's computer system are the customer's account numbers at merchants, utilities, or other third parties the customer may wish to pay.

Each merchant is assigned a payment code, which is known only to the bank and the customer. Whenever the customer wishes to make a payment, a command is entered into his personal computer with the amount to be paid.

A payment can be scheduled up to 30 days in advance, or instructions can be given to the bank to send the payment every month for the same amount.

Local churches should move rapidly to accommodate their members in this process.

- *Balance Inquiry.* Customers can contact the bank's computer 24 hours a day to determine the balance on their checking or savings account. Further, the amounts due on loans and current rates on certificates of deposit are available whenever the customer requests.

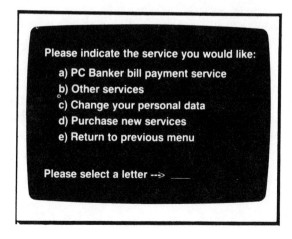

• *Funds Transfer.* The customer can also give instructions to the bank using their personal computer to transfer funds between United Jersey accounts. For instance, customers can make monthly payments to an installment loan, mortgage, personal credit line, or IRA.

• *Checkbook Ledger.* All payments processed through electronic bill payments or funds transfers are automatically entered into the checkbook ledger. In addition, paper checks and deposits can be entered into the checkbook ledger in order to keep the electronic checkbook complete. The balances in the customer's account are automatically calculated when electronic payments or any direct entries are entered.

• *Updating Family Budget.* Having completed bill payments, the Home Information System may then be used to update the family budget. Each payment is entered with a payment type such as food, housing, utilities, dental/medical care, transportation, clothing, and insurance. Whenever necessary, the customer can view his actual payments against the family budget initially programmed into the system. The system in budget control is not limited to payments completed through the personal computer system. Cash transactions as well as other funds transfers may be fed into the computer for transaction memory retention and recall purposes.

Future services to be offered by United Jersey Banks include home financial management, in which customers can apply for certificates of deposit or personal loans directly from their home. Also, the customer will be able to view his checking account activity at his home computer. This information will include check numbers, amounts, and descriptions of items paid by the bank.

A "Pony Express" is obsolete as grade-school children become familiar with the menu printed herein and families move to computer processing. The local church cannot survive without plastic currency and computer processing.

13

New Thoughts on Old Subjects

IT TAKES MONEY to raise money. While most people are convinced of this and accept the premise as a valid truth, it is generally followed up in far too limited a way both in the concept and in the resources for financial development.

Traditionally the average congregation thinks of development cost in terms of the Every-Member Canvass. It begins with the resources that are generally available without cost through the denomination. Then it may proceed to adding other desirable items that are available at minimum cost. The third step is to include postage for one or two mailings with one, perhaps both, under a third-class mailing permit. When the event is over, one is surprised that we expect to raise so much with so very little. The miracle of our expectancy lies in what we actually have achieved. No nonprofit organization can match the church on the local level in development costs. Usually they are as small as one-half of 1 percent! Nowhere can that be duplicated. With a little more expenditure, however, greater resources may be available. The $64,000 question is: How much more? Add to this the further question: In what direction should it be spent?

Probably the most important question we face is: How does one gain experience in proven procedures? The answer to this is: There are a number of ways. Opportunities are legion. But many are costly. In fact, perhaps too costly for most local churches. How, then does one begin?

We can begin with opportunities already available. Recall that college president of a small Midwestern institution from Chapter 2 who shared in every fund drive that came to his city. He learned where the money was. He learned that those who give are the fund raiser's best prospects. Also, he learned how to raise money. Each experience provided new lessons at no cost to him or to his institution.

Regardless of where you are, there are development plans in the making and development procedures in progress. Become a part of them. There are many things that you can gain from them:

• *First,* you can gain a knowledge of proven, accepted, and tested procedures. All are built on broad experiences not dissimilar from those of the local church.

• *Second,* you can gain insights into the science of philanthropy under which the program is structured.

• *Third,* you can become familiar with the tools and procedures used in the campaign.

• *Fourth,* you can gain personal experience in the design of a campaign that you can use throughout the rest of your life.

There are conferences, seminars, and workshops in which you can enroll. Several invitations to professional events are on my desk at this very moment. One involves five days at $1,400. Another involves three days at $900. Too rich? Perhaps. Then try this suggestion for size:

Every two years the Commission on Stewardship of the National Council of the Churches of Christ in the U.S.A. offers a National Conference on Christian Philanthropy. It is a three-day conference in which the very best leadership in the nation is provided for seminars and workshop experiences. Inasmuch as it is underwritten by the stewardship divisions in the member denominations it is modestly priced. In fact, registration is under $200! Leading the conference are such giants in the field as Robert W. Dahlke, president of the National Catholic Development Conference; James M. Frick, vice-president—public relations, University of Notre Dame; Maurice E. Gordon, executive director, National Methodist Foundation for Christian Higher Education; Gerald and Doris Salinger of Audience Analysts, Inc.; Ronald L. Streibich, director of development, Northwestern University; and Conrad Teitell, editor of *Tax-wise Giving.* At the same time you will rub shoulders with some 200 persons sharing the burden of philanthropy and development from every corner of the nation. Other similar events are conducted by the National Consultation on Financial Development at an equally modest price.

I have spoken to many about these opportunities, even in multiple-staff situations, and usually the attitude is negative. Their assumption: "There is nothing there for us." Actually there is a great deal there for you, and just one idea may bring more resources to your local church than the total annual budget.

Seminars, training events, and workshops are continually in progress under the auspices of the denominations and our ecumenical organizations. Yet those most needing them seldom enroll. To pass them by, however, represents a luxury the local church can ill afford.

There are other opportunities as well. Put your name on the mailing lists of fund-raising organizations. Invite samples of materials prepared by commercial firms for fund-raising ideas. Write to institutions in development programs requesting copies of their literature. Each year brings new ideas. Each experience brings new forms and designs.

Correspond, too, with your denominational leadership, its foundation, stewardship department, agencies, and institutions. You can call their resources "junk mail" if you choose, but each will be sharing with you the tested implements for effective communicating and development that are in reality their lifeblood. This is a pivotal decision toward developing resources.

Resources, too, are as close as your radio, television set, and magazine rack. Follow each carefully. Daily there are ideas you can use, procedures you can follow, tools you may implement to turn the world upside down. A pivotal decision toward developing resources is the decision to view critically those things at your fingertips that may be touched by the Master's Hand to bring you and your parish a step closer to the Kingdom of God.

There is another suggestion meriting consideration. Pastors dine with parishioners all year long. Even when it is their idea and they have a project to advance, most usually it is done at the member's expense. This should not be. The pastor and those on the development team should have resources available out of a discretionary fund for breakfasts, luncheons, and dinners. When presenting proposals the proposition should never be made at the prospective donor's expense. What salesman would take a prospect to lunch and expect him to pick up the tab? Whether we think of developing financial resources or resources of talents, reasonable funds should be available to meet the cost of these events. In the pastoral ministry these resources were never available to me, and generous contributors absolutely refused to let me take funds of this type from my family budget. They always paid, whether it was from their personal budget or business expense account. I was ever in their debt when the task required that they should have been in my or the local church's debt. Hundreds of times this element limited my capability to consummate an arrangement that could have been most beneficial to the local church.

When staff or leadership is to meet with potential donors, why do the prospects need to assume the cost of the arrangement? If donors are to pick up the tab, why do not all donors share in it? In other words, why not allocate a sum in the annual budget for this purpose? How much?

Cost will vary from person to person and parish to parish. Breakfasts are the most economical, luncheons often the most feasible in terms of cost and time, and dinners frequently the most desirable. Suppose, as a minimum, the initial budget allocation is to provide for five guest checks each week. Subtract the weeks of vacation, holidays, and conferences, and probably thirty-five weeks' allowance would do the work. This would require funding for one hundred and seventy-five meals. Assuming that the pastor or responsible leader will share in this program we should perhaps increase the head count from one hundred and seventy-five to two hundred and fifty. Assuming that one-third would be breakfasts at four dollars per person, one-third would be lunches at five dollars per person, and one-third would be dinners at twelve dollars per person, we are talking about a little over one thousand dollars a year. This I would consider reasonable for the average parish. As the parish increases in size and affluence the figure should also increase. If this is an impossibility from the local church budget, think of it in terms of project support.

Another area of our financial life that needs rethinking is that of collection procedures. The offering has a central place in Christian Worship and certainly it is an integral part of liturgy. We must concede, however, that few interpret or understand it as an act of worship; for most of us it is nothing more than a collection occupying time with instrumental or vocal music until something more important happens. Although it is considered by many to be a high point in the worship service, major support for most congregations does not come during the services of public worship and this will be increasingly so in the future.

Pastors and church leaders insist that the offering occupies a central place in worship and no liturgy can be complete without it. Yet the act of worship itself is often a denial of the very theological premise they reverence. As an example: How often have you attended a service in which the act of dedication followed the receiving of gifts? In good form and taste the ushers have processed to the chancel to receive the offering plates and in due form they moved down the aisles for the receiving of gifts. In good form, also, they returned to the chancel for the dedication of gifts. However, the offering plates approaching the chancel were empty! The parish officers, anxious to count the morning offering, probably insisted that the ushers empty the collection plates before returning to the chancel for the presentation of gifts in order that the counting procedure could take place at the earliest possible moment.

Worship ought to be honest? If it is important to dedicate gifts through an act of consecration then it is equally important that the gifts be there for dedication.

The blessing of the gift and those who give is equally important. In the Centennial United Methodist Church in St. Paul, Minnesota, the offering is presented at the chancel by the ushers and a selected usher of the day, representing the congregation, offers the prayer of dedication. The First Presbyterian Church in Honolulu, Hawaii, has the offertory prayers given regularly by the trustees; a different trustee is appointed for each service.

The pastoral leadership in a church of three thousand members in a Chicago suburb is distressed by my attitude that every worship service need not include an offertory. They insist that the offertory be an integral part of worship in every service—except the early service at the eight o'clock hour on Sunday mornings. Because they have difficulty in recruiting ushers for this early service the procedure is for the offerings to be placed, informally, in a collection plate located on a central table in the narthex of the church. There is no announcement of the offering procedure nor is there a prayer or act of dedication. However, a careful survey of the congregation made clear three things: First, the offerings received at the eight o'clock services provide the largest percentage in number of gifts to number of persons sharing in worship at that service. Second, the per-capita size of the gift is larger than those received at the two major worship services later in the morning. Third, worshippers expressed a deeper appreciation in sharing as they present their gifts on a table in the narthex than when presented through a steward in the corporate act of worship.

As a young boy in Bethany Evangelical Danish Lutheran Church in Denver, Colorado, I was impressed in seasons of festivity as communicants marched to the chancel, around the altar rail and the rear of the altar to place their gifts on the altar as personal acts of presentation and dedication. This procedure is most appropriate at Advent and Christmas, regardless of whether the architecture provides a high altar in a formal antiphonal liturgical setting or a communion table before the sacred desk. It is also highly appropriate in connection with stewardship enlistment when announced intentions and funds-transfer authorizations are a part of a service of public worship.

Two pluses for the offering as a part of each service of public worship are:

First, the collection of gifts and presentation of offerings are a means of involving persons in the service of the church. In the Westminster Presbyterian Church at Hot Springs, Arkansas, husband-and-wife teams share in the receiving of gifts. In some churches it is youth: all boys, all girls. In some churches men; in a few churches, women. This need not be discounted. For some the procedure of the offering is their unique way of serving the family of faith.

Second, families who have programmed the church into their budgets through funds transfers tend to provide supplementary support through the presentation of gifts. Regular, generous transfers of funds on a monthly or quarterly basis will provide the support the church needs and do much to place Christ's Mission in proper perspective. Pushbutton giving, in fact, may ultimately provide the greater resource. But let us remember: The mission of the church is to make Christ known to the family of God. Unfortunately, the ability to make Christ known is contingent on the resources available for mission from the supporting members in the household of faith. I never cease to marvel at the potential of that support, and the needs across the nation and around the world cause me to be ashamed at how little expertise we exercise in church-funds development inasmuch as we have not yet come of age in the fiscal era of which we are a part. It is time to be alert. It may be later than we think.

The receiving of a gift and dedication of the same does not conclude an organization's responsibility. The story of Jesus and the healing of the ten lepers is known by every lay person across the church today. We first learned it in Sunday school, found it emphasized again and again in Christian Endeavor, and we could hardly attend a worship service in the course of two years without hearing a sermon on the theme. Ten lepers were cleansed. Only one returned to say "thanks"!

It is a paradox indeed that we preach and teach the art of thanksgiving and neglect to exercise the art in terms of those sharing most generously with the church. We have been so determined to treat all members alike. We boast that a pledge or failure to pledge, pay or failure to pay, will make no difference to our pastoral concern, our pastoral ministry. Not only do we treat those who do not pay as though they pay; we treat those who pay as though they do not. This, in my opinion, is the greater sin.

How do we say "thanks" for generous, regular support?

• Many churches follow promotion exercises in the Church School by sending a personal letter to each of the officers and teachers who have served faithfully through the preceding year. Committees responsible for recruiting staff attest that these expressions of appreciation facilitate their efforts in favorable responses to serve again.

• A step beyond this is a similar letter to those who in the course of the year have made a commitment and kept it. No reference need be made to its size, the frequency of payments, or method by which the assumed obligation is met. A simple note to the effect that the pastor has learned of the commitment in support of the parish and the fact that it had been kept, enabling the organization to meet its obligations and exercise its witness to the community, is most helpful.

• A second appropriate letter, following the Every-Member Canvass, is one expressing appreciation, on behalf of the staff and officers, for pledged support for the ensuing year.

• The treasurer, when mailing the financial statement, could well include a personal note, or notation on the statement itself, to the effect that the recipient's support is deeply appreciated.

Two other items of correspondence come to mind:

• If, at the conclusion of the first quarter, there has been no payment on a pledge, and a pattern of giving has not been established by a family over several years, it would be proper for the chairman of the stewardship or Every-Member Canvass committee to write a letter of appreciation for the commitment. The person writing the letter may also suggest that there may be a misunderstanding of the commitment and in the event that the commitment has been misinterpreted, a communication should be sent to the financial secretary at the earliest possible moment. Remember: This is a thank-you letter; thanking the person for a commitment. The letter is also a confession by the organization that the intent in the commitment may have been misinterpreted. The blame of delinquency is assumed by the institution and not ascribed to the donor.

• When the pledge payment period exceeds the third quarter, and there is considerable arrearage in payment, a second letter may be addressed to the person making the pledge, thanking him for his commitment and suggesting that a readjustment might well be made in the commitment in order that the officers may be in a better position to make a valid projection on anticipated income for the end of the year. Here you will invite a restatement of the original commitment for the benefit of the institution. In reality it becomes a benefit to the contributor as well. Thoughtfully and prayerfully the communication should carry the message: We appreciate your support, we understand your situation, we want to help.

Probably no really adequate method has yet been devised for saying "thank you" to those who remember the church in their wills and those who have established Unitrusts and Annuity Trusts for the benefit of the local church. A church is not always aware of those who have written the church into their wills, of course. And there are others who would not wish to be publicly acknowledged. But here are some hints and clues worth considering:

• The Bethany Presbyterian Church in Milwaukee, Wisconsin, designates one Sunday each July for the recognition of memorials, wills, and bequests. Invitation is given to families and friends of deceased members and benefactors in the church, from over the preceding year, to attend the service. A summer date has been selected to facilitate travel and vacation schedules for persons interested in the particular occasion.

In the course of the worship service a member of the Session proceeds to the lectern to read the names of those who have left funds to the church through their wills and those who have been memorialized through special gifts. In each case the assignment of the funds, and in some cases the amount, is included in the report. Examples are funds for local mission, general mission, or for items to be used in the church, such as a chapel organ, set of hand bells, a public-address system, pulpit appointments, etc. Recognition also includes sums given to endow the church's program.

• A Book of Remembrance as a central, permanent record of wills, bequests, trusts, and gifts is always appropriate and would make an additional step in a program of recognition. I believe, too, that a central plaque capable of accommodating fifty or one hundred names, as persons are remembered through gifts, would be in order. If there are reservations concerning the installation of such a plaque or marker in the sanctuary, certainly it could be placed in the narthex or in one of the social rooms in the local church.

Mt. Sinai Synagogue, in Middletown, New York, had such a plaque. They went a step further in their program, as is frequently done in the Jewish community. Lights were installed with one bulb adjacent to each name. On the anniversary of the person's demise the light was turned on and prayers were offered for the dead. Generally Protestants are not exercised to offer prayers for the dead. Indices noting anniversaries may be in order, however, and this may be another consideration.

If one prefers not to go to this length in such recognition, a good

Thank You!

THE SMITH STREET UNITED CHURCH

gratefully acknowledges your gift

in memory of

_____

whose name will be inscribed in

The Book of Remembrance

10001 University

Jonesville, Maine 10001

_____, 198__

_____

Secretary

Donor's certificate acknowledging receipt of memorial gift.

addition to the service in Bethany Presbyterian Church might be to read the names of those persons who, in the course of the preceding year, have included the church in their wills. This would do much to encourage people to remember their church as they write or revise their wills.

• The issuing of certificates suitable for framing may be a part of the memorials, special gifts, Unitrust, Annuity Trust, and Wills-Emphasis Program. The certificates are not expensive, are deeply appreciated by many, are sometimes displayed and become a permanent acknowledgment of record that for others will be placed in a safe or safety-deposit box. The presentation of the certificate is the church's responsibility; the utilization is at the discretion of the donor.

In Remembrance

THE SMITH STREET UNITED CHURCH

gratefully acknowledges a gift

from

_____

in memory of

_____

whose name will be inscribed in

The Book of Remembrance

10001 University

Jonesville, Maine 10001

_____, 198__

_____

Secretary

Certificate sent to family of person memorialized.

Prior to the restructuring of the United Presbyterian Church in the U.S.A., the Board of Christian Education provided an award in the form of a pin and certificate for Associates in Christian Education. The award, presented as an honor, was given in recognition of service to persons selected by an organization or group of individuals who would contribute as much as fifty dollars or more to the Board of Christian Education to honor a person. Sizable sums have been received by the Board of Christian Education this way. This particular procedure would probably not be recommended for implementation in the local church. But it does suggest that certificates of this type may be most helpful in promoting trusts, bequests, and special gifts in the local church.

• One pastor determined to establish a keen pastoral relationship with his people. On annual summer holiday he sent postcards to all his members until it became too great a task. The last year he did this he addressed 637 cards and this was just too time-consuming for a summer holiday. Thereafter such greetings were limited to officers only. Exceptions? Of course. He included greetings to those contributing substantially to the local church. Gifts were sent to those contributing more than $5,000 a year. Costly? Certainly. But even if he were to use a part of his tithe for this procedure, the benefits to the local church would bear evidence that the seed fell on good ground. When he returns as a visitor to parishes where he once served, there are always those who remember the thoughtful gestures. They remember his gifts more than his preaching!

The living word is more important than the spoken word and we will be remembered far longer for the things we do and stand for than for the things we preach. Several years ago I visited a little lady, almost ninety years old, in Beckley, West Virginia. She had lived in a mining community most of her life and related well to the Episcopal Church. Throughout our conversation she spoke enthusiastically of her bishop, the Right Reverend Wilburn C. Campbell, saying: "Bishop Campbell is a wonderful man!" I inquired as to why she had so great a regard for him. Her response: "He acknowledges my gifts so graciously."

More than one person across the church is asking: Where are the nine? Bishops, pastors, and lay leaders can profit much for the kingdom by exercising the art of appreciation.

14

New Models Undergird
New Opportunities

NEW MODELS for financing the local church have come into view. Each one, properly implemented, represents an opportunity to increase support and enlarge mission in the local church. But for each there is the leap from theory to practice, from the idea to the exercising of the opportunity. How often we attend conferences and thrill at opportunities shared from the experiences of the near great. We are enthused, optimistic, and hopeful. But when we return to Homeville, U.S.A., enthusiasm weakens and our optimism flags. It is easier to wrestle with Warsaw's problems in Peoria. It is when we return from Peoria to Warsaw that we meet the test, stand or fall in Christian Mission. Many times we think if only we were somewhere else. But God has placed his hands on our shoulders and in distinct order directs each task as our very own. The test of new models for us lies in what we are able to do with them.

How do we organize to accomplish maximum mission with minimum resources? We must utilize procedures that will provide the greatest benefits. Where to begin is the question.

The *Every-Member Canvass* is the base. It is probably a mistake to move on to other kinds of support until the annual canvass has been solidly established. The tragedy is that we tend to think that the task is done when the Every-Member Canvass is completed. Actually it is there that we must start. Instead of considering it a place of conclusion we must consider it a place of beginning.

It is here that the significance of the profiles for giving begins to appear. Gradually these profiles fall into place. They serve to visualize giving units in terms of their potential for the application of new models. Among them there will be those who should consider the *Gift Annuity Plan.* Those with the financial potential for gift annuities but not as greatly advanced in years, namely, the forty to sixty-five-year age group, will have the potential for the Charitable Remainder Unitrust or Charitable Remainder Annuity Trust. A little study will probably develop three subdivisions or subgroupings.

• *First,* there are those of advanced years for whom the Gift Annuity Plan provides substantial support, regular income, and good tax advantages in terms of gift value, a tax exclusion, and a minimizing of tax on capital gains.

• *Second,* there are the pre-retirement, or life-prime group. While affluent by any reasonable standard, they still require a certain annual income. Variable market values are a threat to their emotional and economic security. These should be invited to share in the Charitable Remainder Annuity Trust. The Trust Agreement will enable them to bypass tax on capital gains, provide gift value for Internal Revenue Service purposes, and permit them a reasonably good exclusion on a sizable portion of their annual income from the trust. As long as they live they can bank on a constant income that will be theirs without risk or fear.

• *Third,* there is the pre-retiree, or life-prime, group very much in growth and steadily progressing into the future with each convinced that he will go higher still. Such persons should consider the maximum benefits that the Charitable Remainder Unitrust Agreement can provide. Their life-style accommodates a risk. While the chance or risk in the Charitable Remainder Unitrust is very small, *there is flexibility in terms of annual income* and certainly in potential for growth. They will risk the variable market. They will settle for a fixed percentage of income providing there is opportunity for growth as well. In the Unitrust they have a constant percentage income, perhaps 8 percent per year, based on the market value of securities held in trust on a particular day each year. They have gift value and have avoided tax on capital gains at the time the trust is established. They have an exclusion on a portion of annual income from the trust each year.

Those interested in Gift Annuities, Unitrusts, and Annuity Trusts are in every parish. They may be few, they may be many—the Every-Member Canvass results will lead you to them. The approach to them ordinarily will require a committee structure. Perhaps the stewardship program is too large to permit this segment of opportunity to be a responsibility of the complete committee. Perhaps the size of the committee is too limited to establish full subcommittees for each area of concern. There can, however, be chairmen and task forces organized to meet the needs for a special approach to prospects in each model grouping.

An alternative to subcommittee or task-force function would be to cycle the program concerns in the Stewardship Committee in such a way that certain areas or models would come into focus at certain times in a year or in a triennium. In this way the work of an entire committee may be directed to a particular area in financial development at a particular time. Year-round emphasis by sub-committees or task forces is the better of the two methods inasmuch as in the cycle procedure there are some who just are not confronted with challenges and opportunities at the most opportune time.

The Wills-Emphasis Program can be a year-round program. "Remember your church in your will" can be included in every Sunday program. Forms for general and designated bequests may be included in monthly newsletters, quarterly reviews, and annual directories or reports. But the effort will prove most productive if a way is found to approach specific prospects from time to time. The Every-Member Canvass and its resultant profiles will provide good leads to those persons who actually fall into the high-potential groupings.

When should a person write or rewrite a will? All persons should prepare a will when they attain maturity. And then the major milestones on the highway of life leave occasions for reviewing and for rewriting a will. What are some of these milestones? The principal ones are:

—coming of age
—financial independence
—property acquisitions
—marriage or separation

—enlargement of the family
—restructuring of life's stewardships (parents independent, parents laid to rest)
—family in flux (members interdependent, dependent, independent and a step away except as heirs)
—vocational progress and change—every change in emphasis or position will require a rethinking of life stewardship and the ultimate distribution of assets and the ordering of liabilities.

Here, too, a counseling ministry will be most helpful. Sermons on estate planning, wills emphasis, and stewardship responsibility for the rest of life are always in order. Periodic emphasis programmed consistently through decades of local church ministry is desirable and essential. Once done is only to begin. There is a need for emphasis again and again.

A review of the profiles constructed for the Every-Member Canvass will also provide leads to those who should consider life insurance and property gifts.

When are prospects brightest for life-insurance gifts? Those who have been good stewards of their resources and mindful of the importance of insuring themselves in the case of misfortune or demise become such prospects as their obligations decline and their nests empty. They will require less protection and will be pleased to exchange the burden of obligation for the resultant advantages of reduced taxes and gift benefits that can come through contributing insurance contracts to their local churches.

Property also is important to their consideration. Through the years the gift of farm acreage to a local church would have made the difference between success and failure in rural America today. Most families sold their farms simply because they did not know that there were other ways to dispose of them. Many would have profited substantially had they turned their property over to their church with or without the privilege of lifetime occupancy.

In the rural areas there are farms, in suburbia there are homes and tracts of land, and in the city there are residential and business properties. Consider this model and share the opportunities with your people. One parish in Florida, located in a high-density condominium area, has assisted many couples by making them aware of the tax advantages to be gained by making a gift of title to their apartment while retaining a donor's privilege of lifetime occupancy. Certainly the local church is not in a position to accept every property offered. A single property gift may ensure the parish mission and enhance capability for ministry in community and nation.

In the church that is alert to their potential, projects for program support will constantly emerge into view. They will literally rise out of the basement and fall from the rafters. They will emerge from the choir loft and leap from the classrooms. Many will simply come out of nowhere. Someone in a pew will get an idea, far removed sometimes from the text of the day, and because of that concern, the need and a willingness to share a project will be born and grow. More projects will arise from circumstances than even the best Stewardship Committee will be able to design or define. And it will be an exciting adventure of corporate faith at work.

A survey of community and parish needs, programmatically, and a review of Federal Domestic Assistance, will marry program ideas to potential funding sources. Potential for program development will emerge from concerns dealing with the underprivileged, exceptional persons, the aged, preschool children, and so on. There is hardly an area of social-spiritual concern untouched by Federal Domestic Assistance available to the religious and charitable organization that will undertake to minister to community needs.

Periodically, surveys should be made in the parish membership and parish community to discover the potential and needs in parish and community life. Periodic surveys, perhaps annually, will do much to enable parish leadership to keep abreast of developments and emerging needs.

While the Stewardship Committee, through a subcommittee or task force, will certainly be involved in greater funding procedures, committee structure might wisely be organized on programmatic detail. The program must be defined before an approach can be made of funding needs and funding potential. This illustrates the importance of the Stewardship Committee's relationship to the programmatic committee of the local church. In the Presbyterian system there is a Session and Board of Trustees in each parish. The Session is concerned with program and spiritual life. The Board of Trustees is concerned with property and finance. Some parishes have turned to a unicameral system in order to merge the two to make for a greater compatibility. Either together or separate, there must be a good relationship in both areas to sustain a satisfactory balance between program and resource.

Ultimately we come to the annual, biannual, triennial or quadrennial budget. The appearance of the budget will change considerably as these emerging new models for financing the local church are more fully utilized. Programmed giving through funds-transfer systems will tend to level income, with fewer highs and lows, to a higher level than has been experienced historically in the church. Support will be more generous and more consistent than local leaders have known before. There will be less risk in establishing budgets and projecting cash flow. Funds will be committed and programmed through family fiscal procedures that will bring the church into proper focus as family budgets make family commitments. As commitment deepens, financial commitments increase and individuals progress with a deeper devotion to the Master and the mission of His Church in these times.

Through more adequate communication in parish and community the congregation will become more knowledgeable of the church's mission, and the parish will relate more closely to the community and community needs. The fellowship of the concerned will not be restricted to those holding parish membership. It will include the involved and believing community. As leaven in the loaf, the parish mission will penetrate every facet of life. It is only in this way that the righteousness of God may rightfully cover the earth as the waters do the seas.

We may be concerned that these potentials do not exist for us in the parish where we are or where we serve. They will exist only in our hearts and minds so long as we permit erroneous conceptions to go unpunctured. Certainly it is time to let the air out of the balloons of inflated assumptions we have projected on the basis of invalid premises.

"Penniless churches in a cashless society" need not be the epitaph for organized religion in the twenty-first century. A sound financial base is as close as the bank card, checkbook, will, trust, project, and/or grant. As these become a part of our programming and planning, the vista of the future will brighten with hope.

Index